6-7-10

To my aunt Alberta's hairdresser, Phylis

Carmel C. Solano

# THE END
## *of the*
# ROW

# The End *of the* Row

**Carmel C. Solano**

Copyright © 2013 by Carmel C. Solano.

| | | |
|---|---|---|
| Library of Congress Control Number: | | 2013904859 |
| ISBN: | Hardcover | 978-1-4836-1207-2 |
| | Softcover | 978-1-4836-0663-7 |
| | Ebook | 978-1-4836-0664-4 |

All rights reserved. No part of this book, *The End of the Row*, may be reproduced or transmitted in any form or by any means, electronic or mechanical, including photocopying, recording, or by an information storage and retrieval system—except by a reviewer who may quote brief passages in a review to be printed in a magazine, in a newspaper, or on the Web—without permission in writing from the publisher. For information, please contact Carmel C. Solano, 2200 Berkshire Dr., Fort Collins, Colorado 80526.

Although the author and publisher have made every effort to ensure the accuracy and completeness of information contained in this book, we assume no responsibility for errors, inaccuracies, omissions, or any inconsistency herein. Any slights of people, places, or organizations are unintentional.

This book was printed in the United States of America.

Rev. date: 03/15/2013

**To order additional copies of this book, contact:**
Xlibris Corporation
1-888-795-4274
www.Xlibris.com
Orders@Xlibris.com

# CONTENTS

Acknowledgments ........................................................... 7

Introduction ................................................................... 11

Chapter 1   My Move to Colorado Beet Fields ........................... 15

Chapter 2   Moving Back to New Mexico ................................. 28

Chapter 3   The Wind and Dust of Amarillo, Texas .................. 33

Chapter 4   The Colorado Fields Again ...................................... 49

Chapter 5   The Adolescent Years of My Life ............................. 67

Chapter 6   Rites of Passage and Off to the Army ...................... 78

Chapter 7   Finding My Way Back from the Army .................... 83

Chapter 8   Finding My Lifelong Friend and Moving On ......... 87

A modified quote from an unknown author. ................................ 97

# ACKNOWLEDGMENTS

Judy, my wife, for her patience and allowing me
the time to write my story

My belated sister, Susan Lopez, for her encouragement
to write and publish my book

My daughters, April, Penny, and Judy, for their support,
encouragement, and curiosity

Betty Aragon-Mitotes, for helping me with fund-raising
and recognition to document history

*Le dedico este libro a los obradores que trabajaron en
las labores de los Estado Unidos*

A special recognition to the Fort Collins, Colorado Museo de Tres
Coloña for incorporating my story as part of the history of Fort
Collins Latino history

"*The End of the Row* captures the real-life experiences and story of an incredible life journey. Solano's story goes in depth to help better understand and raise awareness of educators, counselors, teachers, administrators as they work with migrant farm workers. This book is also a story full of humor, emotions, life challenges, and the resilience and sacrifice of a father fighting to make a better life for his family."

*Rich A. Salas, PhD*

"Carmel has talked about this book for years. Often, while sitting in his barber chair, I insisted that he complete a publication. This book tells it like it is—scars and all. *The End of the Row* has a historical, a poignant, and a true portrait of a man that tarried through the hard times of being a migrant worker yet made something out of nothing. He is an example of success for all Latinos that are in doubt. If you don't give yourself a chance to do the impossible, you will miss the chance of your life to do the incredible. This book exemplifies that true character and vitality of Carmel by telling the compelling story of this man's life."

*Ray Martinez, Former Mayor of Fort Collins, Colorado*

A special thanks to Ray Martinez for his mentoring, guidance, and helping me publish my book. Without his insight and experience in writing and publishing many of his own works, this book would not have come to fruition. Ray's orchestrating and managing the process made my publication a smooth ride. I appreciate his interest and concern for documenting history.

Besides being a customer since 1974, I've watched Ray grow in the community from his law enforcement days through his three terms as the mayor of Fort Collins, Colorado, to working in the private sector and simultaneously hosting his own live talk radio show. I'm thankful and proud of the work he has done on this publication and his contribution to Fort Collins.

*Chuck Solano*

# INTRODUCTION

I was inspired to write this book by a couple of things, i.e., my profound interest in history and self-improvement. I was lucky to pass the entrance examination to join the army with only a sixth grade formal education. Thrown in with draftees with law degrees and teaching certificates, engineers, and college students, I was aware of my insufficiencies in general education.

During a two-year tour of duty in Bamberg, Germany, I discovered the post library. In the military, there is no such thing as not having anything to do. I found out that if I walked around with a clipboard in my hand, I could sneak into the post library and loaf. In the beginning, I looked through *Life* and *Saturday Evening Post* magazines. One day I picked up a book titled *Kinsey's Report on Human Sexuality,* and I thought to myself, "Wow!" I then started to read textbooks such as math, English, science, history, and geography. Two years later, without attending any classes, I tested and passed my GED (General Education Diploma).

I am not a voracious reader, but I like to read and am a prolific reader. Early on in life, I recognized the importance of reading. Reading not only opened up a whole new world for me but also opened doors of opportunity. This is a value I have tried to instill not only in my own children and grandchildren but also with the young people during the many lectures and presentations I do for the school district and throughout the community.

I grew up in a poverty-stricken and dysfunctional family. It is important for me that future generations know how their family grew up and where they came from. They need to know what their heritage was like, where they traveled, and the characteristics of their social life. Reflecting back on my seventy-plus years, I am in awe about my own life experiences; it was one hell of a ride.

I have been in the company of great men and some *lowlifes*, learning what is good and bad from both groups. Being book smart is important. A person can achieve knowledge through teachers or sneaking off to the library. It depends on how eager a person is to learn. I immersed myself in politics, education, and public service. During the civil rights movement, I was encouraged and marched to City Hall with Federico Pena, Richard Castro, and Rueben Valdez. Later, Federico became the mayor of Denver, Richard Castor became state representative, and Rueben Valdez became the director of DORA (Department of Regulatory Agencies) in Colorado. Respectively, Bill Lopez, a former city councilman; Blair Keifer, a Fort Collins businessman; and Dr. Abel Amaya from Colorado State University were instrumental in forming my core values and made me the person I became.

During another phase of my life, I was part of the group that boycotted table grapes, lettuce, and Coors beer. I took part in many community organizations such as the following:

A candidate for the Fort Collins City Council
The president of the Chicano advisory group for Poudre School District
A member of Human Relations Commission Department for Fort Collins
The president of Parks and Recreation Board for Fort Collins
Member of the Fort Collins Museum Board
Treasurer of PTA of Saint Joseph School
Vice president of LULAC (League of United Latin American Citizens)
Member of Jaycees and Sertoma clubs

You will notice that at the beginning of each chapter, I list a quote in Spanish. These are quotes that I grew up with and were part of our friends and family dialogue whether we were joking around or serious about one thing or another.

You can do anything you set your mind to do.

Buena Suerte
*Chuck Solano*

# CHAPTER 1

## My Move to Colorado Beet Fields

*No le menelles la cola al gato.*

It was a dark, stormy night, and suddenly a shout rang out. I was just born with the help of a *partera* (midwife). Every good story has a good opening sentence, so here is mine. We lived in Tucumcari the first four years of my life. With World War II starting in December 1941, toy soldiers and weapons were very popular. A young friend of Mom and Dad's babysat me a lot, and we played with my cardboard toy soldiers. Tucumcari, New Mexico, is a small town of about two thousand residents and east central New Mexico. Our country was just coming out of the Great Depression, and everyone was beginning to finally work once again. Dad was working at the ice plant, and Mom worked as a maid in a motel. There wasn't any industry in town other than motel work. The town of Tucumcari lies halfway between Chicago, Illinois, and Santa Monica, California, on Route

66. So a lot of the travelers would stop overnight. The town survived because of the motel business.

Dad was classified 4-F by the military, so he didn't have to go into the military. He was the youngest of three boys and one girl. One of my dad's brothers went into the army, and the other one went to the penitentiary and had just got out. His sister was a cook in a hotel restaurant. Dad's brother, Pablo, wasn't a hardened criminal; he just chased a man all around the neighborhood with an ice pick. He couldn't catch him, but he managed to cut the man's back to ribbons. On another occasion, my uncle Pablo went to the *pen* for bootlegging whiskey. They had a reputation for being *canallas* (scoundrels).

In 1944, when Dad decided to move to Colorado, I had a sister one year younger than me and a brother three months old. We traveled by train to Colorado that had more soldiers than civilians on the train. Dad and some soldiers drank whiskey and played dice during the whole trip. In Trinidad, we needed to switch trains, but we missed our connection because Dad was drunk. From the train depot, we had to walk across the tracks to another train. We carried some of our luggage, and I started to whine and complain about carrying too much. Dad took one of the paper bags I was carrying, thinking it was trash, and threw it down an embankment as we walked on an overpass. Mom realized he threw my sister's black baby rag doll away, so she had to climb down the embankment to retrieve it.

We reached our destination, which was a farm owned by Jack Frost, eight miles east of Eaton, Colorado. Mom and Dad started thinning the farmer's sugar beets. I was only about three and a half years old, Dolores was two years old, and GG, the baby, was about six months old. The farmer's wife kind of looked out for us while Mom and Dad were in the field working.

Uncle Nick and Clara Lujan lived a little ways down the road. One day I was at their house and found some matches and accidentally started a small grass fire. My Aunt Clara put the fire out by beating on it with a kitchen mop.

The following fall, we moved down the road a couple of miles to the Myers' farm. We lived in a two-room shack covered with corrugated iron steel that was colder than a *well digger's behind* in the winter. Dad brought home a puppy once, and the poor dog froze to death on a cold winter night. It was a tough winter, and because Dad couldn't find work, he spent a lot of time drinking wine in Eaton at the Spanish colony named "Rag Town." We ate a lot of beans and potatoes, but once in a while, we had meat, and it was so good that I would even eat the fat; but to this day, I can't stand the fat around a piece of meat.

Mom bought me a nice sport coat with leather trim with gloves to match, but I seldom wore them because we never went to town. An old man that was our neighbor named Cuco often walked into town; and on his way back home, Dolores and I made sure we were outside playing, knowing he would always give us a piece of gum or candy.

When Mom ran out of smoking tobacco, I would walk up the road and find cigarette butts for her to grind up and roll a cigarette with rolling papers. We moved to a farm near Milliken the following year where I started first grade. Dad worked for the farmers all summer while Mom canned some fruits and vegetables so that the next winter wouldn't be as rough compared to the previous one.

That year I remember some damned pervert scared the hell out of Mom. Some afternoons he would park down the road, get out, and open his fly. He never did it when Dad was around; otherwise, Dad and his brother, Uncle Nino, would have knocked the hell out of him.

My Uncle Nino and his family lived down the road about half a mile. Living in our neighborhood were my mom's brother, Uncle

Albert, and my grandmother's brother, Uncle Ben Velasquez, and family.

Junior and Teo, Uncle Nino's boys, had lived with us during the winter before. They suffered hard times right along with us. Dad and Uncle Nino did a lot of drinking in Rag Town, and Mom did the best she could with what she had. The boys later told their mom that they were mistreated by my mother because they were not given enough to eat while the rest of us ate like fat rats. They even accused Mom of spending their money that was given them by their dad; hell, he never gave them any money. Uncle Nino and Dad spent most of their time and money in Rag Town. There were times when we wouldn't see them for days because they were out drinking wine.

I started first grade that winter of 1945 in Milliken. I didn't know how to speak English, but it was going to be fun to learn. My first day on the school bus was greeted with a question by someone wanting to know if I was a boy or girl; I was dressed in a snowsuit, and all you could see were my eyes and nose.

I remember the few times going to town with Dad to buy groceries at a little store called Christy's. Dad gave me a nickel to buy Baloney bubble gum. I wore bib overalls, and while at the store, I asked Dad to buy me some waist pants or Levi's, thinking that would make me a big boy.

One time, Dad walked home from Johnstown in a snowstorm. He and a friend, Joe Medina, were out drinking; and their car broke down. When Dad got home that night, he and Mom must have argued; for some reason, he kicked the kitchen stove and knocked it over. Next day, I saw him resetting the stove upright and putting the chimney pipe back in place.

One night, Mom and Dad went somewhere and didn't take Dolores and me. They must not have gone too far—probably to my uncle's house down the road, noting that they would be right back. I don't know how long they were gone, but I sat on a chair by the door and stared at a kerosene lamp because I was scared to move or look at anything else.

We next moved to a farm between Eaton and Ault. The farmer's name was Bill Roman. I stayed with my Uncle Nick Lujon and Aunt Clara to finish the school year in Milliken. A month or so later, I joined the family. About this time, JG, also known as Jose Guiermo, was around a year old.

Dolores had a pair of boots that I really liked. I repeatedly tried to make them go on my bigger feet, but I was sure disappointed that they wouldn't fit. My Uncle Ben Velasquez must have moved to that area because I remember Abby, his son, visiting us and having a lot of licorice gum called Charcoal.

I also remember my mom's brother, Albert, and his wife, Alberta, visiting for a few weeks. It was about this time I remember Dad thinned beets for the farmer. He fed sheep and hauled straw on a horse-drawn wagon. On one occasion, when he was loading manure with a pitchfork on to the spreader, I thought I would be nice to the horses, so I got a big chuck of manure and set it in front of them so they would have something to eat. I asked Dad why they wouldn't eat what I gave them. I remember his smile and saying, "Caballos no comen su mierda."

The other hired hand was an Anglo that had a boy about my age. We played together, but we couldn't communicate because I didn't speak English and he didn't speak Spanish. When I started school in the fall, I only knew two English words, which I had learned from the boy. They were "rocks" and "somersaults."

When I went to school the first day, the school bus came by the farm, and I was supposed to get on the same bus to get home after school. There were five buses, and the bus number on our route was 4. Dad even wrote the figure 4 on a piece of paper so that I would get on the right bus. Well, my first day at school in Ault was a disaster. When I wasn't able to ask for permission to go to the bathroom when nature called, I pooped in my long johns. And then when the kids would look around, trying to figure out who stunk, I would pinch my nose and say "phew" and point at the kid next to me.

When it was time to go home that afternoon, I got confused by the numbers on the buses. Rather than get on the wrong bus, I walked the four miles out to the house. For a long time after that, Uncle Albert wouldn't let me forget that I had pooped in my pants. He also took pleasure in making fun whenever I wore a pair of riding britches Mom had bought me. He called them my *guarda pedos,* which means "fart savers."

Dad's mom died the winter just before Christmas, and Dad went by himself to Tucumcari for the funeral. Mom put up a Christmas tree for the holidays and decorated it with homemade ornaments. She strung some popcorn and made paper chains with colored pieces of paper and put some candles on the tree.

Abby Velasquez, our cousin, came to visit us one time and suggested he light the candles on the tree. He lit three or four before the tree started to burn. We managed to put the fire out but not before half of the tree burned. Mom turned the burned side toward the wall, and we never attempted to light the candles again.

Dad was supposed to be gone for only a week for my grandma Rita's funeral, but he stayed six weeks. When we started to run out of groceries and coal, Mom got worried. That winter, we had one of the worst blizzards since 1923. Mom kept the potatoes in the bottom drawers of a dresser we had in the house and even those were freezing. When she cooked potatoes, she would have to cut and discard the frozen parts and cook what was left. Things got pretty rough for us, so my Gampo Cypriano Martinez, Mom's dad, took us to live with him and his second wife, Felica, in La Salle, Colorado. We lived in a one-room house in his backyard.

I almost forgot that we also lived in a one-room shack in West Greeley. Our landlord was Charlie Bueno, and he had a crush on Mom, but he was an old man, and so she didn't like him.

Grampo Martinez called my sister Dolores "a little perico" or parrot. She was about five years old when we lived in his backyard. We had a pot belly stove in the middle of the room to warm the house. One Saturday, after we took our usual baths in a laundry tub, Dolores was standing too close to the stove drying herself. She accidentally dropped her towel, and when she bent over to pick it up, it burned her butt pretty bad. She still might have a scar from that burn. After that, Grampo would call her *perrico cola quemada*, which means "parrot with burned bottom."

Finally, after about six weeks, Dad and his brother, Nino, showed up. Dad sent my uncle to our house to announce that he was finally back from New Mexico and to find out if they were welcome. I could see Dad standing under a big cottonwood tree in an empty lot next door. My uncle told me to go talk to my dad, but I was kind of embarrassed and didn't really want to. Suddenly my uncle reached out and grabbed me by the seat of my pants and forcibly took me to where Dad was standing. I kept backing away from him, but eventually, he reached down and hugged me. I hugged him back because I knew I was happy to see him.

We lived in La Salle for a few months that winter and rented a house from Candelario Lujan and a basement from a lady we called "Kata" where they liked to make home brew. One night, his sons and I took the hinges off the door to the root cellar where they kept their beer locked up. We were only around seven or eight years old, but that quart of home brew we stole got the five of us a little woozy.

When we lived in the basement apartment at Kata's, a friend of mine, Fermin Gonzales, and I got a hold of some chewing tobacco. We must have swallowed some of it because we both got pretty sick. We hid in a corn field across the road from the house and moaned and groaned with stomach cramps and vomited. Dad found out about the tobacco, so for punishment, he made me sit down on a little bench; then with his pocket knife, he cut a pretty big chunk of tobacco and told me to chew it. I cried more than I chewed.

In the spring of 1947, we moved to a farm east of Ault. It was a typical two-room house that farmers built for their field workers. A kitchen with a wood burning cook stove, a cupboard for dishes, and a wash stand with a mirror and basin to wash your face and hands. There was usually a round oak table, maybe two chairs, and an orange crate to sit on. The bedrooms had one bed, a floor model radio that would need a bobby pin on the back to play, along with a couple of over-stuffed chairs. Dolores and I slept on a mattress thrown on the floor. Mom, Dad, and the little one slept on the bed. We used kerosene lamps for light and cistern outside for drinking water. A tin laundry tub was our bathtub on Saturday nights. A wash board and cheap lye soap was Mom's washing machine.

There was an outside toilet around thirty yards from the house. It had one little hole for kids and one big hole for adults. In the backyard, there was also a *basurero* (dumpster) where we threw rubbish and trash. In the same area was a wood pile with a one sided ax.

Our toys were all broken that were either left there by the previous tenants or workers or ones that we would get at the county dump that had been discarded. Ah yes, I remember the weekends when Dad would say we're going to the dump. That was our family outing on weekends. We would pack a lunch and go spend the day scavenging for toys, furniture, magazines, and any usable items we could find. We even had our favorite dump sites because some were better than others. This was the lifestyle in every farmhouse we lived in until I reached the age of seventeen and enlisted in the army.

I entered the third grade that year and became friends with Fred Gonzales and Victor, kids that liked to steal pinion nuts and candy.

I missed the school bus once and had to walk home. I didn't mind the walk because it was only about a mile to the farm. I had a friend who lived on the edge of town, and he had a two-wheel bike that I wanted to learn to ride. I lost track of time while we were playing, and eventually I saw Dad walking toward town. I knew I was in trouble then, so I started walking home until I met him. I knew he was mad because all the way home we walked in silence. When we went in the house, he took off his belt and told me to take my pants off. He wet the belt in the wash basin and gave me a beating I'll never forget.

Nena was born about this time. She was a cute little tyke with a little flat button nose. They named her Mary Magdalene, but we called her Nena. There was a baptism party where the *compadres* and friends came. Naturally, there was a lot of food, pop, beer, and liquor. Mom and Dad knew this couple, May and Felix, who were real close friends. They were so close that they gave Nena to them because they promised to give her everything that Mom and Dad couldn't afford financially. They had Nena for about a week when Mom and Dad had a change of heart. Mom cried every night for her baby, and finally, Dad walked from the farm to Ault and then to Pierce, Colorado, which was about seven miles each way; we didn't own a car then and then walked back with Nena in his arms. They lost their friends, Felix and May, that day.

The next summer, we lived south of Ault, and that is when Fidel, Dad's sister, Aunt Julia's son, came to stay with us. He was about seventeen, and to me, he was a big husky, dark, curly haired man, and I really liked him. I wanted to be big like him when I grew up. He drank a lot of milk and ate a lot of eggs that the farmer would supply for us. He had a Brownie camera and took a lot of pictures of the family that summer. I have one picture of my mom, dad, and myself out in the beet field that I had enlarged thirty years later and displayed it as my degree in agriculture.

GG was about four years old and started to show signs of being spoiled, rotten kid. He associated bad with black. If he didn't like something, to him it was black. If he didn't like a toy, it was black; if he didn't like someone, he was black. Dad thought he was cute; to me he was a darn pest.

Once Dad brought home a little duckling, it was a nice little pet that we let run loose in the house. We had him a few weeks until one night I put him near my mattress where I slept. I must have rolled over in my sleep and smothered him because he was dead the next morning.

We thinned out beets and did the weeding for that farmer, then Fidel went back to New Mexico, and we moved to a farmhouse north of Ault. A man by the name of Raphael Beltran lived with us and paid—or was supposed to pay—for room and board. He and Dad were drinking buddies that had met in a bar in Eaton. He was a wet back who couldn't speak English, and with a song book he carried with him, he taught me how to read in Spanish.

You've probably heard or read about the dust storms that were common during the Great Depression in the 1930s. We had one such storm while we lived at that house. It looked like a huge, dark cloud close to the ground that slowly rolled in from the north and darkened the day and made it look like night time. Mom put wet towels around the doors and window sills to keep out the fine dust. It lasted about an hour or so, and when it was over, the sun came out, and everything was calm and clear.

Jobs were pretty scarce in the winter for unskilled labor like Dad and Raphael. A family friend that lived down the road was also having a difficult time trying to feed his family. It was very hard to get welfare from the state unless you were a resident for at least a year. The men would walk along highways and roads, looking for empty beer or pop bottles to turn in for the deposit. They stole a couple of sheep from farmers over by Fort Collins, and thinking back, sometimes all we had to eat was meat and tortillas with no vegetables to go with them. One time, they came home real early in the morning with some ducks, rabbits, a guinea hen, and about thirty or forty chickens. They took them to Denver and sold them to a poultry market.

One evening, they went to a liquor store in Ault to sell the bottles that they had found during the day. Dad's two companions waited in the car while he went in to redeem the bottles for grocery money. There was a man in the store buying a bottle of liquor, and when he took some money out of his front pants pocket, he accidentally dropped some folded bills on the floor. No one saw it fall except Dad, and he casually walked over, covered the money with his foot, and prayed that no one else had seen it fall.

When he related the incident to us later, he said a team of horses wasn't going to move him because he had seen a twenty in that stack of bills. As the customer turned to leave, he bumped into Dad and had to walk around him to get by because Dad wouldn't budge an inch. When the man was gone, Dad pretended he dropped a cigarette he was smoking; and then when he reached down to get his cigarette, he also picked up the money, carefully, so that the store clerk would not see. He set the sack of empty bottles on the counter; the clerk counted them and then gave Dad about fifty cents for the deposits. Outside in the car, there was another paper sack full of bottles, but Dad got in the car and drove off.

His companions were mystified why he wouldn't take the rest of the bottles into the store. On the way home, on a country road, he pulled over to the side and took out the wad of money. He counted out $100! All three men were speechless for a few minutes, then he divided up the money, and they went and bought groceries and went home.

The following weekend, Dad took all of us to Denver in his Model "A" Ford. Driving down Larimer Street, the back door opened accidentally, and my brother GG fell out and landed in the middle of the street. I yelled out and picked him up. Fortunately, he wasn't seriously hurt, except for a goose egg bump on his forehead. He was four years old, and Dad had him spoiled anyway, but after that incident, for the rest of the day, that kid could have anything he wanted. That same day, Mom and Dad bought clothes and toys in second-hand stores on Larimer Street. They bought us sandwiches, candy, and pop. They had a few beers in some of the bars.

My sister, Susan, was born that year, and she had a cute little peanut nose, so we called her Pinny. In the spring, we moved to Milliken into Uncle Nick Lujan's one-car garage. He had a five-acre truck farm with hogs, chickens, and a couple of cows. I got the job of feeding the animals every day and got two dollars a week for it. I bought a used bicycle for five bucks to get around that summer.

Mom and Dad thinned beets and did other types of farm labor around Milliken. On Sundays, when the local semipro baseball team played in town, everyone would go watch and have a picnic after the game. The players and spectators would go to the one bar in town, and it wasn't unusual to see a fight after they drank awhile.

Dan Thornton was a candidate for state governor that year, and one day, he came to town to campaign. He gave his speech to some people in front of the post office and handed out candy bars to the kids. My friend Louie and I stood in line and got our candy bar. Then we thought we would get smart and try for another candy bar. We took our shirts off and stood in line again and got another candy bar. We figured that without our shirts, they would not recognize us the second time.

There were two girls in town about my age then: Dolores Salazar and Alice Belo. Alice was kind of small, feisty, and tough with you if she didn't like you. And Dolores was a bigger girl but nice. I kind of liked her. My cousin Annie Lujan was a couple of years older than me, and her sister Jenny was about sixteen. On Saturdays when they got back from Greeley after shopping, Annie had little bags of candy, but she wouldn't share. All week she would hide her candy and eat a little at a time, but she wouldn't give me or Dolores any, unless my Aunt Clara would see her eating some and us not. One time when she wasn't home, I went in their house for some reason or other. I saw the sack of candy and took it. Dolores and I ate it all.

# CHAPTER 2

# Moving Back to New Mexico

*Dime con quen andas y te digo quen eres.*

In the fall of that year, Dad and I went to New Mexico with an uncle that was moving down there. We rode in the back of a truck with all of the furniture. Going through Denver, we stopped and saw Mom and Dad's *comadre,* Susie. She had baptized my sister Pinny earlier that year. We stayed overnight in some motel near monument because the truck broke down. When we got to Tucumcari, we moved in with my Aunt Julia, Dad's sister. Mom followed a few weeks later with the rest of the kids. I started school in a school that had burned down the year before. I only had to go half days. Half of the class would go in the morning, and then the other half would go in the afternoon.

One kid, by the name of Tony, got in the habit of picking on me. He was bigger and stronger than me and made life miserable for me every day. One day, he waited for me in the school yard after school. He slapped me around, threw me on the ground, and had me face down with my arms locked up behind me. I was scared and mad because he was stronger. I was defenseless. That is until I saw his knee real close to my face. I reached over, latched on to the inside of the knee with my teeth, and bit as hard as I could. He let out a yell, released my arms, and started screaming. I bit him so hard I drew blood, but he never bullied me again.

One afternoon, another kid that I had made friends with, and I were playing at the local park. There were two Indian boys about our age also playing. Some older boys came by and started taunting and picking on the little Indian boys. My friend and I thought we would join in the fun. We yelled and whooped like Indians doing a war dance. At the time, *Red Ryder* and *Little Beaver* were popular in the movies, so we called them "Little Beavers" and had a good laugh. That is, until the older boys left. As soon as they left, those two little Indian boys came after the two of us. We ran, but they caught us; one got my friend, one got me, and they beat the hell out of us. We went home with our noses bleeding and our tail between our legs like two whipped pups.

My friend and I were once playing in a ravine at the edge of town. Digging around in the sand, we found two old cavalry swords from the horse and buggy days. We walked into a local candy store, and when the store keeper saw the swords, he asked us where we got them. We told him we had found them, and he immediately offered us fifty cents worth of penny candy each in exchange for the swords. We had no knowledge of antiques, so we agreed to the trade not knowing that he was taking advantage of us. What goes around comes around, so I'm sure someone in his lifetime took advantage of him.

Our family moved to Amarillo that year. Mom and Dad figured that it would be best if Dolores and I stayed with Aunt Julia and finish out the school year. Things were fine for the first couple of months, but as the old say goes, "familiarity breeds contempt." My cousin, Jessie, who was pregnant was very temperamental with us and got cross very easily. They laid some pretty strict rules on us that were hard to take, but we were expected to obey without questions. We couldn't have friends over to play, we had to clean the house and wash our own clothes every day, and we couldn't go to play at friend's houses very often. Our entertainment was mainly reading comic books and an occasional movie once in a while. Television was so new that I hadn't even heard of it.

A friend of mine, Ted Chavez, introduced me to smoking, and we would cough and choke trying to smoke Pall Malls. My Uncle Nino's sons, Junior and Teo, came from Santa Fe and visited us at Christmas time. Junior was thirteen years old, and Teo was twelve. I was eleven, and Dolores must have been about ten. When they came to visit, I had the impression that my aunt kind of favored them a little better. If I asked if we could go to a movie, she would say no. If Junior or Teo asked, she invariably would say yes. Jessie was the same way. Fidel, her son, didn't show any favoritism. Junior and Teo's parents were separated then—that might have been part of the reason. They wore engineer boots that were popular with the kids, and they had nicer clothes than Dolores and me. I can remember them talking about shining shoes and "picking" for spending money in Santa Fe. "Picking" was a term used for shoplifting. My aunt and Jessie thought it was cute and funny when they talked of picking, but if I even thought about it, I would have caught hell.

We often went downtown to the five and dime stores. While one of us would talk to the shop keeper to distract her, the others would pick stuff small enough to go in their pockets. Then we would go to a movie, sit in the balcony, and smoke a whole pack of Pall Malls between the three of us and see who had "picked" the best. I was resentful with my aunt for her preference to the boys, so when she sent me to a little neighborhood store where she had credit to buy milk or eggs or something, I would add some rolls or donuts and eat them all before I got home.

Coming home from the store one day, a couple of brother my age started bullying me. They pushed me around trying to get me to fight, but I wouldn't do it. I walked away from them until I got to the end of the block. I picked up a rock about the size of an egg and threw it at them. I didn't think I was going to hit any of them. But boy, the small kid didn't know what hit him. When the rock hit him on the head, it bounced twenty feet. He went down for the count like a sack of potatoes. We later became friends, and their dad informed me that he thought I had killed his boy that day.

Christmas to me that year wasn't a real happy one. I missed Mom and Dad too much when we were with them in Amarillo and me and Dolores in Tucumcari. I was also resentful of Junior and Teo because they didn't have to go to confession and Holy Communion like Dolores and I. But it was OK for them to go ask for Christmas goodies from the neighbors. It was the custom for kids to go on Christmas morning knocking on doors and asking for candy. People would give out candy and cookies just like people do on Halloween.

"My home from 1947-1948, just northeast of Ault, Colorado."

"My sisters: Doi, Nena, and Pinnie standing by my dad's 1932 Chevy."

# CHAPTER 3

# The Wind and Dust of Amarillo, Texas

*Cada chango a su mecate.*

After Christmas, the boys went back to Santa Fe, and we went back to school. Jessie got meaner, probably because of her pregnancy. One day, she beat me with a belt and left some strap marks on my behind. I wrote a letter to Mom in Amarillo and told her about it. The following weekend, Mom and Dad came and took us back to Amarillo.

In Amarillo, we lived next to Dwight Morrow Elementary where I enrolled in fourth grade. We lived in a two-room ramshackle house. It was unpainted, run down, and sat next to the alley. The streets were unpaved, and with the wind flowing constantly, it was always dusty.

I joined a neighborhood boxing club for something to do. I'd go once or twice a week to skip rope and hit the bags. After a few weeks, the older boys talked me into getting in the ring with Mene. Mene had been in the club about two years. He had two older brothers that had competed in Golden Glove tournaments. The club was going to box and other boxing club and probably wanted to see how I would do in the ring. Mene weighed about twenty pounds more than I did and had more experience.

I had to borrow some tennis shoes and trunks. The gloves they put on me were so big I could slip my hand in and out without placing them. The tennis shoes were two sizes too big. We were to box three two-minute rounds. I only lasted two. That kid hit me at will, and I couldn't hit back. After punching me in the nose and making my eyes water, I got mad and tried to kick him. When the referee told me not to kick, I got mad, slung my gloves off, and walked out of my oversize shoes and went home humiliated. That was the end of my boxing career. Later I got in a school yard fight with Mene. There was no referee there, so I could kick, scratch, and bite. I whipped him good.

We lived in Amarillo a few months, then we moved to Boise City, Oklahoma. Dad's brother, Uncle Pablo, and his wife, Dominga, lived there. We moved in with them in a railroad section house. Uncle Pablo worked for the railroad. I guess Dad was trying to get a job with the railroad.

We also had another distant uncle, Uncle Margarito, that had moved from Clayton, New Mexico, to Boise City. He lived on the north edge of town. I didn't like him real well. We visited him in Clayton once when he lived on a ranch before he moved to Boise City. He had a grandson named Jose Almansa. His parents lived up north in Elkhart, Kansas. He was about fourteen years old, and I was about eleven. One time, he came to stay with Uncle Margarito and was left alone while Uncle Margarito and his wife went someplace for an overnight visit. Mom and Dad took me over to keep Jose company overnight. That SOB woke me up in the middle of the night fondling me to satisfy his homosexual desires. I woke up wondering what the hell he was doing. When he saw me awake, he went back to bed. That scared the hell out of me. I didn't tell anyone, but I grew up with an intense hate for gay people and beat the hell out of them whenever I could. Years later, I came to understand that pedophiles, who are criminals, and gays, who just lived a different lifestyle, were not one and the same.

Once again, Dolores and I were left with relatives when our parents moved to Elkhart, Kansas, where Dad worked for the Union Pacific Railroad. We stayed with Uncle Pablo and his wife. My uncle never had any children of his own, so he couldn't cope with an eight—and eleven-year-old. They were strict disciplinarians and wouldn't let us go play with friends, and we couldn't bring friends home to play. They didn't beat us physically or were overly mean; they just wouldn't let us do anything that most children liked to do.

If it snowed, we couldn't play in the snow. If it was sunny, we couldn't go out because we would get dirty, and we could never go downtown alone or with them. One weekend, when Mom and Dad were coming to visit, my uncle took me into town in his old pickup. He bought me some candy and pop and gave me a few coins in change. He told me how well they had treated us kids and how much he enjoyed having us with him. He said he didn't want us to tell my folks any lies about them treating us bad in any way. He felt guilty, and I thought what a hypocrite he was. I don't remember if I told my parents or not, but I know Dolores and I went to Elkhart with my folks before school let out that year.

In Elkhart, our house was a one-room railroad section house down along the railroad. There were three other workers like us with the same type of house. The foreman had a big four-room house.

Tornadoes were very common in that part of the county, and I remember seeing two different ones in the same day. The closest one ever got to our house was one that touched the edge of town right across the street from us. It was terrifying because it sounded like a freight train roaring right through the house. Mom put us children, Dolores, GG, Nena, Penny, and I, under the dining table while she and Dad burned holy palm reeds and sprinkled holy water throughout the room. I think that was the first time I saw my dad pray.

The town bully didn't take long to get after me in Elkhart. My brother GG, who was seven at the time, had met him and got along fine with him. Years later, I found out they even sneaked a smoke now and then together. But that dang kid was making life miserable for me. Every time I went to the store where we had credit, I'd run into him, and he would slap and push me around. He was a year or two older, so I felt I needed help. I started putting in my pocket one of Dad's pocket knives. I finally got to use it when he was pushing me around. I only scratched him a few times on the arms, but he quit bothering me.

I was walking home from school one afternoon, and one of the town barbers was standing in front of his shop. As I passed by, he called to me. I stopped, and he asked if I wanted a job as a shoeshine boy. I started shining shoes on Saturdays and after school. I got fifteen cents a shine, and he let me keep all of it. I made one to five dollars a week, which, to an eleven-year-old kid, was pretty good spending money. As soon as I made a couple of dollars, I'd go into a variety store and buy shorts for thirty-five cents or shirts for about a dollar. *New!* Or I'd go to a small cafe for lunch on Saturdays. I think Peggy Lee had a number 1 hit entitled "Mockingbird Hill" because that song always seemed to be playing on the jukebox every time I went in.

One Saturday, when Mom and Dad weren't on speaking terms, probably because Dad had gotten drunk the night before, Mom asked me to go to the store for her. On the way out, I asked her if I could buy some candy. She said, "Oh, ask your dad." Dad was outside chopping wood, and when I asked him, he answered sarcastically, "Buy ten pounds if you want." Well, I took him seriously. At the store, I bought Mom's order of food: milk and baloney. However, the clerk thought I was nuts when I told her I wanted ten pounds of candy. She weighed Snickers, Milky Ways, and penny candy on the produce scale to up ten pounds of candy. Mom was shocked when I got home with all of the candy, but she was mad at Dad, so she didn't send it back. She still remembers that incident and laughs about it.

There was one theater in town, and on Saturday afternoons, my dad's foreman sons and I would go to the show and see Donald O'Conner in "The Milk Man" or Gene Autry in "Back in the Saddle Again." After the show, we would go have a root beer float. The movie cost fifteen cents, and the root beer float cost fifteen cents.

That year, I met my first love. I thought my third grade teacher was the most beautiful woman that ever lived. I would sit in class and dream of riding off in to the sunset with her, like John Wayne and his girl did in the movies. I would make excuses to go to her desk during class just to be near her. But I had to settle for a little girl named Mary to call my girl. I think she always had some candy. Her other boyfriend had more material things, like bicycles and toys. His name was Charlie Brown.

That summer, I went to school and learned how to be an altar boy and to learn how to pronounce Latin so I could sing in the choir. GG got involved with the Nazarene Church and had more fun with their activities. By the way, Mom had no idea he had joined until she got a note inviting her and Dad to a program that the children were going to put on. Mom said that the people from the Nazarene Church were much friendly and did more for us than the Catholic Church.

I joined a Cub Scout troop that summer, but I never did get to buy a uniform. All I did was make a paddle boat out of a piece of one by six inches board and a rubber band. One weekend, Dad,

Dolores, and I got on a train that went to Boise City. All it consisted of was a passenger coach, mail car, and a caboose. From Boise City, we went with another couple in their pickup over to Dalhart, Texas. We stayed overnight at their relatives. The next morning, we went to the Trail ways bus station.

The pickup had broken down and needed repairs that would take a couple of days. While at the bus station, Dad bought Dolores and me a one-way ticket to Tucumcari. The owner of the broken down pickup, who was to be our host for the night, and Dad were in the bus station coffee shop waiting for our bus. About an hour before our departure time, Dad and I went to the restroom. He told me that no matter what happened, Dolores and I were to get on the bus. He was very emphatic about it and reassured me everything would be OK. Just be sure to get on the bus. I said OK, and we went back to join the others in the coffee room.

After a few minutes, Dad excused himself, saying he was going down the street to a store to buy something. As it got closer to our departure time, I started worrying because Dad hadn't come back. Those other two men also started to wonder why he wasn't back yet. As I was standing by the ticket counter, I happened to look down on the floor and saw a dollar bill. I picked it up and put it in my pocket looking around nervously thinking that any minute someone would come up and tell me to give back their dollar. I also got panicky because the bus started to load luggage and passengers, and Dad was still nowhere in sight.

Those two men kept looking up and down the street to see if he was coming. I thought of not getting on the bus and waiting for him until he got back. But I remembered what he had told me "that no matter what happens, be sure to get on the bus." We got on, and as the bus left the terminal, I wondered what had happened to Dad. The bus reached the outskirts of town, and ahead, I could see the black ribbon of highway heading across the Texas panhandle. About five miles out of town, a lone hitchhiker flagged the bus to a stop. The driver opened the door, and I sighed with relief when I saw that it was Dad. He looked back at the passengers, and when he saw Dolores and me, he gave us a big smile; and after talking to the driver, he came back and sat across the aisle from us.

The reason for this cloak and dagger stuff was that Dad had offered to pay for half of the expenses for the ride to Tucumcari. When the pickup broke down and needed major engine repairs, the men expected Dad to pay half of the cost. Dad thought he was obligated to pay only for half the cost for gas and oil. I guess he figured this was the only way he could get out of having to pay for the engine repairs. I wonder if he ever saw those men again.

In the fall of 1952, we moved to Tucumcari so that my brother Raymond could be born there. Dad quit his job with the railroad and moved so that Raymond could be born in New Mexico. Not long after Raymond was born, we moved back to Amarillo. We stayed that winter. One spring day in April 1953, I was told we were going to Michigan to thin sugar beets. Dad had been drinking at a local neighborhood tavern and had met a man that took field workers to Michigan every summer. One rainy spring morning, this big truck covered with a canvas tarpaulin came to pick us up. We were the last family to be picked up, so we got the worst spot on the back of the truck. There were already five families on the truck; ours made six, which totaled ten adults and seventeen kids ranging in ages from six months to sixteen years of age.

We were allowed to take a couple boxes of belongings. As we got into the truck through the crawl door at the back of the truck, everyone looked upon us as intruders. It was crowded, stuffy, and there wasn't much room. Mom and Dad made a bench of the two boxes that belonged to us, and that's where they sat. They spread a blanket on the floor for the little ones to sit on. The only place for me was the truck's spare tire which lay close to the crawl door. The tire was my bed and chair for the next four days until we got to Michigan. Two other families had their own transportation.

One had a 1946 international pickup, and the other had a beat up 1941 Ford.

Two days out, somewhere in Missouri, the Ford broke down. The family just abandoned it and got in the pickup truck with the other family. It also had the back covered with a canvas. In it were four adults and eight kids, plus their belongings. Whenever the trucks stopped for gas, we would all line up to use the restroom. Imagine the gas attendant coming out to gas up the trucks and seeing thirty-eight people lining up to use his restroom. At one of the stops along the way, Dolores and Nena were left at the gas station. They were the last to use the restroom, and when we left; nobody noticed they were missing. We got the truck driver to stop by yelling and beating on the cab. As we were turning around to go back, a car drove up with the gas attendant and the girls. He had seen them both crying, put them in his car, and raced to catch up with us. Mom was relieved to get her girls, but I think the attendant was more relieved to get rid of the whole bunch of us.

Somewhere in Indiana, the two families in the pickup truck became separated from us and were lost, catching up with us in Michigan a day later. A friendly police department in a small town had put them up for the night. They provided blankets and mattress and allowed them to sleep in empty cells. They provided breakfast the next day and even gave their dog a can of dog food.

Finally, we arrived in Michigan and found housing on farms north of Port Huron. Each family was assigned to a sugar beet grower by the Great Western Sugar Company. We were assigned to a farmer near the town of Sandusky. Our house was a three-room house. Great Western Sugar Company loaned us eating utensils, and the farmer provided some furniture. Our mattresses were mattress covers stuffed with straw. Our farmer had about twenty-five acres of beets, and we signed a contract stating we would thin them for eleven dollars an acre. Each family signed a similar contract with their respective farmers.

The northern lights are a magnificent phenomenon, but if you've never seen or heard of them, they can scare the hell out of you. Mom and I went to the water pump one evening to haul buckets of water. On the way back to the house, the northern lights started their majestic shimmering. Mom exclaimed, "Oh my god," and Dad asked what the matter was. I think Mom thought the world was coming to an end and told Dad to look outside at the sky. We went out, looked, and came back inside. He told us to calm down and then explained to us what we saw.

A row of beets when planted come out of the ground like radishes. Our job was to thin the little plants with a hoe until there was one plant every ten inches. You start at the beginning of a row to hack away at the little plants until you have the smallest clump you can leave. Then with a free hand, you pull the rest of them until you leave one strong plant. You do this up one row and come back on the next row. Up and down, up and down, day after day. You had to be at least fifteen years of age to thin beets with a hoe; that law was never enforced if the farmer was satisfied with your work. The older workers would use a long handle hoe and have a small child on hands and knees behind them pulling the plants. Everybody else would cut the hoe handles off to make it short enough so that when you stooped over, your free hand would be close to the ground to remove the clumps.

My sister Dolores was eleven, so she helped Mom, while I thinned with a hoe. I daydreamed a lot to get through a ten-hour day. I was slow and couldn't keep up with Mom and Dad. Sometimes Dad would try to embarrass me by telling me that I was slower than a woman. To embarrass me further, he would send me home about half an hour before we stopped for the noon meal. "You work like a woman," he would say. "So go start a fire on the stove, start frying potatoes, and set the table for the noon meal." I would hand over my hoe to Dolores and take off. He did that a few times to see if I would work a little faster. His theory didn't work. At about 10:30 a.m. every day, I would start asking him if it was time for me to go and start lunch. He eventually delegated that job to Dolores, and I lost my so called "woman's" job.

We thinned beets from May to around the first of July. When the beets were all thinned, families packed up and moved up north near Travers City to the cherry orchards to pick cherries. The farmer provided us with a dairy barn for living quarters. We cleaned the barn as best as we could, stringing wire with a blanket over it to create little "apartments" for each family. I slept outside on the truck on a bed roll with about eight other boys. Mom and Dad and the little ones had a mattress on the floor in the barn. We cooked our meals on a two-burner camping stove. Privacy was unheard of in those close quarters. At night, you could hear men and women fight, and there were enough young children whimpering to keep everybody awake. The restrooms were outdoor privies, and only the women were allowed to use them. The men and boys just went into the woods whenever nature called.

There were hundreds of other migrants in the area to pick the cherry crops. In the mornings, we would all load up the truck, men, woman, and children and converge with other migrants at an orchard. Within a couple of days, the cherries would be picked, and we would move to another orchard. We were paid about twenty-five cents for every ten pounds of cherries, and I had a good day if I picked twenty buckets a day. An adult could pick twenty-five buckets a day and earn approximately $6. Between Dad, Mom, Dolores, and me, we made approximately $10-$15 a day.

On Sundays, we would all clean up and go into town. The men would sit in a bar and drink beer; the women would buy groceries, and the kids would go swimming in Lake Michigan. After the cherry crop was picked by mid-August, we moved south near Lansing to pick cucumbers. We didn't make much money picking cucumbers, but it gave us some work before we moved to Ohio near Limon to pick tomatoes. We moved into a camp on the Ohio, Indiana state line near Wilshire, Ohio. Our housing facilities were pathetic. My family was assigned a sheep herder's camp trailer. The trailers were designed for a single person in mind and about the size of a fourteen-foot camping trailer, the farmer's expected a family of seven to live in it. We were fortunate that the farmer had some hog pens in the field nearby. We cleaned three or four of the A-frame huts and used them as sleeping quarters for the boys and some of the adult men. Some people had to sleep in cars because it was getting too cold at night to sleep outside under the stars. The tomato crop was the last thing to pick before we headed back to Texas for the winter.

Most of the families by this time had hopefully saved enough money to buy a good used car. It was a status thing to go back to Texas in your own automobile instead of the back of the truck. The newer the car, the more status you had. People were buying 1949 Chevys and Fords.

We bought a 1933 Plymouth. Dad taught me to drive it on the pasture behind the camp. He would sit me on the driver's seat, and he would stand on the running board. He showed me how to start it and put it in gear. When I got going, he would jump off, and I would drive in circles around the pasture. I would rest my elbow on the open window and pretend I was cruising Main Street. I learned to drive well enough to get to town on country roads.

Dolores hopped on the rear bumper one Sunday when I was taking Dad to town. He was drunk, and I didn't see her climbing on. She held on until I picked up a little speed, then she either slipped or jumped off. She wasn't hurt bad—only bruised and scraped.

After the tomato crop was picked, it was time to head back to Texas to pick cotton. Most families had cars, so the truck wasn't too full. The trucker asked Dad to drive his new Ford with our '33 Plymouth loaded on the truck. Dolores and some of the trucker's children rode to Texas inside the car on the back of the truck.

We got back to Texas about mid-October and picked cotton near Lubbock. We picked cotton for around six weeks and didn't make any money. For some strange reason, my family couldn't pick fast enough. An average adult could pick seven hundred to one thousand pounds a day. Dad, Mom, Dolores, and I would pick eight hundred pounds a day. They paid us one dollar per one hundred pounds, so it wasn't worth it. Another group of migrants joined us, and in the group, there were two twin boys about my age. They started picking on me and making life miserable. They'd beat me until I went home crying. Dad tried to get me to fight back but couldn't. The camp adults were always egging those boys on, and being twins, everyone thought they were cute.

Around the first part of December, we moved to Amarillo for the winter. I entered the fourth grade again. We moved in to a five-room single-level adobe house with four other families and Arthur's at twentieth. Each family rented a room and used the same restroom. It was a flush toilet, but half the time it didn't work, and we would have to go to other people's restroom. The house sat on a corner lot and at one time must have been a grand house. Now it was a ramshackle run-down rooming house with a tin roof and no grass or trees. Our room was about 10 by 15 feet and rented for $15 a month. When you walked inside, there was a small gas stove on the right. On the left was a small cupboard and table. Lengthwise across the ceiling was a wire that had a couple of blankets draped over it to create some privacy for Mom and Dad's bed. The kids would sleep on a mattress on the floor that was rolled up and pushed out of the way during the day. Dad got a job as a dishwasher in a small diner, and part of his pay was the food that wasn't sold during the day. He would come home with open cans with gravy, mashed potatoes, some kind of vegetables, and some kind of meat.

Dad had taken to drinking a lot at this time. Instead of just drinking on weekends only, he now was getting drunk on the weekdays also. He was let go from his job and after that he just worked here and there a few days at a time. There were times when he would get behind on the monthly rent of $15. Fortunately, the landlord drank a lot too, and he and Dad were good buddies. They drank a lot of Tokay or Port wine because it was a cheap drink for them.

Christmas came in 1953, and I don't remember having a Christmas tree, exchanging gifts, or having a big holiday dinner.

In those days, a kid could go to the Liberty Theater and see a *Tarzan* or Roy Rogers movie for a dime. A box of popcorn cost a dime and a candy bar sold for a nickel. So if I scavenged empty pop bottles, all I needed was twenty-five cents for an afternoon at the movies.

I got acquainted with Luis and Marcos Sandoval who lived across the alley from us. Their family and mine were economically about the same, and we became close friends. The three of us would go down to the warehouse area near the railroad tracks and steal cases of fruit, vegetables, ice cream, or bread. One of us would distract the night warehouse worker by flipping him the bird, calling him dirty names, and having him chase us. Meanwhile, the others would jump on the dock and pull off a crate of bananas or apples or whatever was handy.

We became known as *callejoneros,* loosely translated as "alley cats." But every kid in our neighborhood was one. We would go to the nice residential section of town and walk through alleys picking up anything usable that people had discarded. We would pick up broken toys, clothes, furniture and take them home and use what we could. We would make the rounds of supermarkets downtown, and in the back of the stores, we would find overripe fruits and vegetables whose parts were still edible. The Nabisco Cookies warehouse employees were nice enough to put broken packages of cookies in a box and sit them in the alley for us. These were desperate times, and even Mom and a couple of ladies in the neighborhood had to make the rounds behind grocery stores a couple of times.

My sister Margie was born that winter, and Mom was breastfeeding her, so she was lucky; she always had something to eat. My brother, Raymond, was a year old, and he had it a little rougher. There were times when all we had to give him was bean broth instead of milk in his bottle. State welfare was hard to get in those days because of laws requiring you to be a resident of a state for a year to qualify. We never lived more than a few months in one place, so we never could get relief.

That Christmas, I got drunk for the first time in my life. At a friend's house, the adults were having a party, and someone bet me a dime I couldn't drink a glass of wine without stopping. Well, I won my dime, but I also experienced my first blackout drunk. My friends took me home stumbling and half walking and put me to bed. Mom found out about it, but Dad didn't. She blackmailed me with that incident for a while. If I didn't do something, or I was slow to do something she wanted, she would threaten me by saying she was going to tell Dad. She had me going pretty good for a while because I was afraid of what Dad would do if he found out.

I dated Cecilia Gonzales a couple of times. I was thirteen, and she was twelve, so no way could I expect to get her parents' permission to take her to a show. I'd meet her and her little brother at a church theater where they showed Mexican movies. We'd hold hands throughout the whole movie until they were wet with perspiration. When I walked them home after the show, I would wonder if she was going to let me kiss her. If she let me, would my lips be too dry, too wet? And how should I put my lips when we kissed?

"My parents and I thinning sugar beets."

"Myself with my siblings: Doi, GG, Pinnie, and Nena in Ault, Colorado."

"My sisters Pinnie and Nena in Kress, Texas, picking cotton."

"My family in Wilshire, Ohio, in 1952 picking tomatoes. My parents, GG, and me."

# CHAPTER 4

# The Colorado Fields Again

*El que no llora no mama.*

We made it through that winter and in the spring of 1953; Dad started making plans for the coming summer. He talked of going back to Michigan or even to Florida to work the fields. We still had the '33 Plymouth that we bought in Indiana. He decided it was good enough to get us to Colorado. The first part of April, we quit school, packed up what we could in the old car, and took off for Colorado. The car made it fifty miles out of town. Dad made arrangements to sell the car for junk. We waited a few days in Amarillo until a trucker from Lubbock picked us up. He had a load of migrants head for Fort Lupton, Colorado, so he gave us a ride. We checked into the labor camp in fort Lupton, but Dad knew his way around in Colorado, so we just went to Johnstown and contracted with Loyal Case to thin his beets south west of town.

The Quintanas lived down the road a couple of miles from us, and they were thinning beets also. They were cousins of ours, and Archie and I became close friends. We would visit each other when we weren't working and go swimming in a reservoir. One day, his sister, Connie, and I decided to cut each other's hair. I cut her hair first and tried to follow her instructions. She said to cut the back until it came to a "V" or a point down her neck and her bangs to her eyebrows. When I finished, she took one look in the mirror, screamed in horror, and then told me it was my turn. We made a mess of our hair, but I think she didn't try very hard after she saw how I cut hers. She wore a bandana all summer and got a silly looking suntan around her face. I had to cut what was left of my ducktail into a crew cut.

Dad had a drinking buddy down the road by Harts Corner. The last name was Vargas, but Dad calls him Chango (monkey). He had a couple of daughters that were chummy with my sister Dolores. I got chummy with one of them and kissed her a couple of times, but boy, was she homely. The man's wife was named Agida, but Mom called her Changa. I think Dad was kissing her on the sly when they were drinking.

Mom was very sick that summer, but she was a strong woman. Years later, she said that she had spit out her tonsils out in the field one day. My Uncle Nino came to visit once again, and he and Dad were constantly drunk. They would be gone for days, while Mom and I would work like slaves out in the field. One day a week I would make a fire in the backyard and heat water in two five-gallon buckets, then Mom would wash clothes in a round tin tub and a washboard.

My Uncle Nino borrowed my Dad's car, a 1936 Dodge coupe, and went drinking one weekend. He was drunk for days over in Eaton or "Rag Town." On the way home, he stopped at a secondhand store in Evans. Some of the used appliances were out on the sidewalk for display. My uncle backed the car up to a wringer type washing machine and, with a lot of confidence, started to wrestle the machine into the car. A salesman came out, saw him, and asked if he could use some help. My uncle said yes, and they put the machine in the car. He thanked the man, got in the car, and as he took off, the salesman told my uncle, "Thanks and come again." He thought my uncle had paid for the washing machine. Even though Mom didn't like for Uncle Nino to come around because of the drinking, she thought that washing machine was great.

Across the road from our beet field, there were about five Braceros, also thinning beets. Bracero was a Mexican from Mexico brought here by farmers to work the fields. The government issued them green cards to come to this country to work. Dad would sometimes act as translator for them and sometimes get drunk with them. Once in a while, I would go to town with them and translate for them. I went to the house they lived in and saw that one of them had written his name and where he was from Mexico. He was from Torreon, Coahuila, and a very interesting place.

That winter, we decided to stay in Colorado instead of going back to Amarillo. Dad got a job at the sugar factory, and we entered elementary school in Johnstown. Dad bought a 1940 Ford sedan that he painted with a brush because the paint on it was pretty faded. At Christmas, we all got some small gifts and groceries from the Salvation Army. Construction slowed down in the winter in Colorado, so Dad didn't work much. Dolores and I worked in the school cafeteria during lunch to pay for our hot lunches in school.

Farmers were constantly improving their farm machinery to make their work more efficient and replace the field worker. Machines were being designed that could pick cherries, cotton, cucumbers, thin beets in the spring, and top them at harvest time. We topped beets for a farmer who was the last one to do them by hand in Weld County. The Johnstown newspaper wrote an article about the farmer being the last one to use migrants to top beets by hand. They should have given Dad a plaque, a certificate, or some recognition, but those turkeys didn't even mention his name.

The following spring, 1954, before the beet work started, Mr. Hayden, our principal, offered me a job to spade his garden and clean his yard. He had some riding horses up at Drake, Colorado, so I strung fence and cleaned corrals for him. He gave me a bicycle one of his sons had outgrown and gave me $2 every Saturday. The first two Saturdays were OK; by the third week, I was going to quit because I thought he was taking advantage of me. Dad owed the school $40 for our books, and he sent a note to Mr. Hayden saying that as soon as he started working, he would pay. Mr. Hayden tore up the note and said that I had paid for them by working on Saturdays.

John Meza was a close friend who was fourteen and in the sixth grade. He and I would steal candy from the stores downtown, and we could beat up any kid in school. We hung with older guys that weren't in school. Paul Gonzales and his brother, Conce, had a real nice 1949 Mercury that we cruised in. We would steal gas from unsuspecting farmers who left their tractors in the fields and then drive to other communities to pick up chicks. On Saturdays, we'd go to Johnstown to the local joints, play the pinball machines and the jukebox, and then try to get a girl to go to the Lonely Tree, a lovers' lane, so we could smooch. A gallon of draught beer cost $1.50 so we would each get one, cruise around, and get drunk.

I once borrowed an ID from an older guy and was able to buy beer at the Dew Drop Inn. It was great to go in, buy a Miller's High Life for thirty cents, and act grown up—that is, until Dad caught me. *Wow!* He went in and read the riot act to that surprised owner. He told her that I was a minor, and she could go to jail for selling me the beer. He told me that if he ever caught me drinking again, he would kick the hell out of me.

On Wednesday nights, the local theater in our small town showed Mexican movies. All the migrants went into town for a midweek break. I didn't consider my family to be migrants because we had relatives that were permanent residents in Milliken and Johnstown.

Sometimes fights would break out between local Chicanos and the Tejanos from Texas.

Archie Quintana, Siguel Velasquez, cousins of mine, and Paul Gonzales Conce were quite a little gang in those days. Most of us carried a knife or a bicycle chain in our pockets for added support in case we got in a fight with other gangs. I had a barber's razor for a while, and then I started carrying a billy club out of a pool cue stick. My dear mom always went through my pant pockets when I was asleep looking for my arsenal. If she found a chain or a club, she would take it and throw it in the outside toiler.

That year, I went to jail for the first time. I stayed in town after school one day and went to catechism class at the local church. After class, while waiting for my ride home, I ran into Herman Sedillo at the Dew Drop Inn. After we spent our change on soda pops and french fries, we were still hungry. He knew a farmer down the road just outside of town that he had worked for on occasion. Herman always got paid by small checks for the spot jobs he did for the farmer. So we decided to write a check made out to Herman from the farmer. I wrote the check for $6, and when I asked Herman what the farmer's name was, he said it was Ritter. Well, it turned out the name was Raider, and the girl we tried to cash it with called the town marshal. We went to the Weld County jail for three days and then went to court where the judge gave us a lecture about the evils of crime. He said it was strange that on one hand, we went to catechism to learn to live well, then went right out and did a bad thing by forging a fake check. He let us off easy because all they were going to do was watch us real close for a year.

In July of 1954, I had my fourteenth birthday. We moved to a farm southwest of La Salle and worked for the Ewings. We picked cucumbers and helped with the potato crop. I got my first real job driving a truck for Mr. Ewing. Dad was real happy because both of us were making a dollar an hour and bringing home two paychecks. Dad bought a light blue '39 Chevrolet sedan. I borrowed the car one Wednesday night and had my first real date. I drove into La Salle and picked up Ramona. She had been a neighbor when we lived in La Salle a few years earlier. I took her to the Mexican show in Johnstown. Not so much to see the show but so that my friends would see me driving down the street with a chick next to me.

In the fall, Dad decided to go to Texas and pick cotton. We loaded up the Chevy with blankets, clothing, and what dishes we could and piled in the car—Mom, Dad, and six kids. Another family from Texas that Dad knew loaded up their '38 Chevy, and together we left for Amarillo.

We tried picking cotton down in Tulia, Texas, but it was the same story. We just couldn't make any money at it. I got a job with a farmer plowing up the cotton fields after the pickers were through. I made more money, at ninety cents an hour, than the whole family did picking cotton. Some of the farmers were starting to use mechanical pickers that year.

We moved to Amarillo for the winter after the cotton was harvested. We moved in to the same apartment house that we had lived in the year before. The rent had gone up to $20 a month. Dad got a job with a roofing company. I found part-time work with an appliance store at sixty cents an hour. My job didn't last but a few weeks, and I'm sure Dad got me fired because of his drinking problem.

We settled into the same poor environment that we lived in during the previous winter. I had a couple of close friends that I hung around with: Luis Sandoval, who was a tough kid; and Phillip Loza, who was kind of mild mannered. I kind of fitted in between the two—not too mean and not too mild. The typical style of clothes was the Pachuco look. We wore baggy black slacks that were tight around the ankles and low around the hips, sporting a gray sport coat with one button, where the sleeve would hang down to the finger tips when you stretched your arms down your sides. A pink shirt and wedge shoes with a white stripe around the soles would round out the outfit. *Oh!* I can't forget our long hair pomaded and combed back into a duck tail. We would dress up on Saturday nights and go to a dance at the church or the dance hall on Cleveland Street. None of us had the guts to ask a girl to dance, but we sure looked cool standing around and eyeballing the chicks.

We would pool our nickels and dimes and get three quarts of grand prize for a dollar. A sign of growing up then was when you could buy your beer by the six packs or case. The older guys would call us the "quart boys." We resented it, but we couldn't afford the cans. Sometimes we would inhale gas fumes from the gas tank on my dad's '39 Chevy and just reek of gas fumes. When questioned about the smell, we just said we ran out of gas and had to siphon gas from one car to another.

One night, we started thinking that teachers had a habit of leaving money in their desks overnight. We broke into an elementary school outside the barrio one night. The three of us, Phillip, Luis, and I, dressed in black clothes and met at a predetermined spot about a block from the school. In a commando type raid, one by one, we walked along hedges and fences and scurried up a fire escape. We pried a window open and got in. I was terrified, but I couldn't show it because that was grounds for being labeled a *gallina* or chicken. We didn't find any money, but we took a record player. We took turns keeping it at our homes and told our parents that it belonged to Luis; he told his folks that he had borrowed it from Phillip, and he said he borrowed it from me.

A couple of months later, we broke into my old elementary school. We felt our way from desk to desk in the dark. Luis was rummaging through a teacher's desk when I asked if he found anything. "Just Kleenex," he replied. Then I heard him mutter, "Oh shit." He was going to blow his nose with what he thought was Kleenex; instead, he had pulled out a hand full of Kotex. We didn't find more than sixty cents, so we went into the cafeteria. We ate a boiled chicken, some chocolate cake, and Jell-O in the dark. The next day, the kids didn't have a hot lunch in school because we ate their dessert and makings for the chicken soup. They put the blame on one of the neighborhood drunks.

Sometimes we would roam around town after curfew, and the police would haul us into the precinct and keep us overnight. After the third time, Luis and I were sent to a detention home for about three days. To me, it was paradise, and I was kind of disappointed when I saw Mom and Dad drive up to take me home. In that home, we had showers and private rooms. One wing was for girls and the other for boys. There were six girls and four boys. We had a central kitchen where we cooked our own meals. The old couple who managed the home assigned me to work in the kitchen with the girls. I was the youngest of the bunch, and the girls got a kick out of flirting with me. They took turns teaching me my duties by standing real close to me and trying to look real sultry into my eyes. We could watch TV until 9:00 p.m. in the kitchen, and a couple of those tall blondes would take turns holding my hand when no one was looking. They would talk of breaking out of that joint and taking me with them, but I didn't want out. I was in hog heaven.

When I got out of that detention home, Luis, Phillip, and I went into our old routine, but we never got caught again. We broke into another school and again didn't find any money. We took a small box of twenty-four little cans of salve that we sold door to door around the neighborhood. We got twenty-five cents per tin and told people it was good for sores and dry skin. We never did vandalize when we did these things. We just wanted a little spending money because we were all so poor. The three of us were real close friends and would share anything with each other. A pack of gum or a candy bar was always split three ways. "All for one and one for all" was our motto.

One time, we were downtown in the bus station, and this old geezer asked us if we wanted a drink up in his apartment. We said sure and went with him to his place. The old bastard was a pervert, and after a couple of drinks of Four Roses Whiskey, he put his arms around me. I backed off and pulled out my chain. Phillip pulled out his chain, and Luis pulled out a knife. That old pervert was about to shit his pants. He started crying, and we debated whether to knock the hell out of him. He was shaking and crying so badly we decided it wasn't worth it and left.

In the spring of 1955, we left Amarillo and went back to Colorado to work the fields. We loaded up the '39 Chevy again, said a prayer, crossed our finger, and hoped it wouldn't break down. It made it all right, and we found work at a farm near Hart's Corner, a few miles out of Johnstown.

Mom and Dad had baptized a baby for Martin Bitela in Amarillo, and the family had come with us. We shared a three-room house with them. Martin had five children, but best of all, he had two boys about my age, and I had someone to chum around with. Victor, whom we called Zorra, was sixteen years old, and Martin Junior was eighteen. But Martin's mentality was only about fourteen.

About three weeks after we had been at that house, the three of us were sleeping on the back of Martins truck when we were awakened by some knocking on the house. My two friends, Phillip and Luis, and two other guys I knew from Amarillo had hitchhiked to Colorado to work for the summer. They had no idea where we lived or how to find us; they were just walking along the highway that night when they saw Dad's '39 Chevy. Those son of guns were just plain lucky the way they found us. They hitchhiked five hundred miles in two days and incredibly saw our car on the second night of their journey.

I was real happy to see Luis and Phillip, and my dear mom didn't hesitate to get up and make the boys something to eat. She provided blankets for them, and we bedded down on the back of Martin's truck. We talked all night about their trip and how lucky they had been in finding us. The next day, Dad made arrangements for room and board for them. They were to pay Mom so much a week, and she would provide food, laundry, and blankets for them. That poor woman would work right along with us in the fields and then go home in the evenings to cook and do laundry for all of us; Dolores was about thirteen, so she helped her some.

Overnight, our family had grown from six kids to ten. On Saturdays when we went to town, we made quite a gang. Luis, Phillip, Ernie, Ramon, Zorra, Martin Junior, and I would team up with my friends in Johnstown. Nobody would fool around with us because if some unsuspecting fool made the mistake of fighting one of us, he didn't stand a chance. We must have made quite an intimidating group by people seeing twelve teenage boys walking into the pool hall on Saturday nights. Some Saturday nights, we would go to dances in Greeley at the state armory, and everyone would move aside to make room for us when we walked in.

The boys stayed with us all summer and worked right alongside of us. We thinned beets, picked cucumbers, and shocked wheat. In the fall, we moved to Herman Carlson's farm near Johnstown to pick potatoes. When the potato crop was finished, it was time for the boys to go back to Texas. They each carried a suitcase, wore new clothes, and had a few bucks in their pockets. When we took them to the Greyhound bus station in Greeley, I had mixed emotions about them leaving. Now we could live with more privacy as a normal family, but we had also had a lot of fun that summer. We promised to see each other the following summer, but I never saw those guys again and often wonder what became of them.

Dad's drinking was getting worse every year, and it was tough going into the winter with no jobs around. We lived rent free, so we just had to worry about groceries and wood for fuel. We had stored about four hundred pounds of potatoes and one hundred pounds of beans and flour, so we always had something to eat. Dad worked three hours a day at $1 an hour, so that disqualified us for welfare.

For Thanksgiving, we ate two old hens I stole from a farmer one late night when Paul and Conce were giving me a ride home. My friends had been talking of turkey and dressing and all the good things they were going to have. I realized all we had was beans and potatoes. So on the way home, I asked Paul to stop near a farmhouse south of town. I sneaked alongside of the road and into a chicken coop and very quietly picked the two chickens off their roost. The chickens were very cooperative and quiet as I put them gently in a gunny sack. Mom knew I had stolen them, but she didn't say anything. The only problem was that they were old hens, and even after boiling them all day, they were still as tough as rubber. Christmas was better, thanks to the Lion's Club. All the kids got a toy, and we got a turkey and the trimmings for a nice dinner.

We had a black-and-white television set, and every afternoon, we would watch the Mickey Mouse Club. I was secretly in love with Annette Funicello, but so was every kid my age. I longed to visit Disneyland, but with a meager existence, I knew it was an impossible dream. My plan for the following year after running sixteen was to work in the tunnels up in the mountains or work in construction. The military was another alternative, but that was a couple of years away. The older guys were joining the military, and when they came home on furlough, they talked about the fun and travel. I was envious. They all seemed to like the service, except for Dolores's boyfriend. He come home on furlough one weekend and didn't go back. Jesse would walk the four miles out to our place to see Dolores and spend the day with us.

On one of his visits, the county sheriff was out looking for him. I went out, and Sheriff Tegman asked if Jesse was around. I told him no, but the sheriff knew he had been to our home and was still there. The sheriff had been a farmer we worked for back in 1948, so he knew our family. He put me in the car with him and a deputy and tried to get me to tell him where Jesse was hiding. I kept telling him I didn't know and hadn't seen him. We drove off in the car driving down the country roads looking for Jesse. When they took me back home, I convinced them that Jesse hadn't been around. As I was getting out the car, the sheriff said, "There's the SOB." Jesse was hunkered down in the irrigation ditch. They drew their guns and went over, pulled him out, and placed handcuffs on him. As they pulled away with Jesse in the back seat, Tegman rolled the window down and told me I was in trouble for hiding an AWOL soldier, and he was coming to get me too. He never did, but I sure sweated for a few weeks.

One day, Dad came home with a big 1949 Buick that he had bought and gave me the old 1939 Chevy. He told me to take good care of it, and I would have transportation. The first thing I did was purchase a can of black enamel paint, a brush and then painted the old car. It didn't take too long before I ruined it. I started selling it piece by piece for spending money. First, I sold the battery, then the tires; and eventually, the junk man from Milliken picked up the whole thing for $10.

Dad would never loan me the Buick, and it burned me up because I felt I had helped pay for it. He would just say I ruined my car, and now I could walk. He was right, but I couldn't accept this explanation. Sometimes Felix Quintana, my cousin, would borrow the car, and I would do a slow burn. I promised myself that someday I would buy my own car, and I wouldn't lend it to my dad.

The winters were much more difficult on a Colorado farm than they were in Amarillo. Without a car for transportation, I would be stranded for days with nowhere to go. In Amarillo, you could go downtown and maybe see a movie or walk to a friend's house to visit. But on the farm, you lived from weekend to weekend. I was lucky if one of my friends came out to the farm to pick me up on Saturdays.

Dad and I spent most of our time chopping wood. When a snowstorm would hit our area, I'd be inside of days until I couldn't stand it. Sometimes I walked the four miles into town for a Coke just to break the monotony. There were no boys' clubs or YMCAs or anything to occupy our time, so we would loaf around the pool hall and get some older guy to buy us some wine. On Sundays, we'd all pitch in and fill someone's tank with gas and cruise to other towns looking for girls. Sometimes the girls' boyfriends would come after us, and either we would have a fight or they would run us out of town, depending on how many they were.

Rock-and-roll music was becoming more and more popular, and so were the gang fights of the fifties. Ninety percent of the fights were over a girl. Paul Gonzales got in a fight with a guy from Milliken over an argument about his girl, Madeleine. And for three years, the guys from Milliken and Johnstown couldn't get along with one another. One night, we got the hell kicked out of us by a bunch from Milliken. We were parked by the gas station in Johnstown about midnight; it was wintery, and the windows in the car were fogged up, and these guys sneaked up behind us. There were five of us and about eight of them. Conce even had a pistol, but he didn't shoot at them. He shot a couple of rounds in the air trying to scare them off, but they just took the gun away from him. Two guys had me on the ground near the front of the car, and every time one kicked me, I would hunch up under the fender and try to break away. I wasn't hurt badly, mostly my feelings because one of my attackers was my cousin, Abby Velasquez. He was drunk and didn't know it was me. Paul and his brother Conce had to get stitches on their heads.

We started carrying a double-barrel shotgun in the car after that night. Weeks later, we saw the Lopezes' Ford convertible leaving town after the bar had closed. Here was our chance to get even with them. We followed them to beat the hell out of the two occupants, but they wouldn't stop. On the road to Milliken, by the sugar factory, they must have been going eighty miles per hour with us right behind them. I realized they weren't going to stop, so I hauled out the shotgun, leaned out the window, pointed the gun, and fired. The first round hit the trunk of the car and peppered it like it had been sandblasted. The second shot I fired missed entirely, and by then, we were approaching Milliken, so we turned around and went back to Johnstown. We laughed and talked of that incident for years not even thinking of the gravity of the situation. I could have killed those two guys.

Another time on a Sunday, at a skating rink in Loveland, I knew there was going to be trouble as soon as the five of us walked in. A young man called Jerry indicated I was the one they were after. One of the older guys on my side suggested we go outside and talk about it. I walked out ahead of everyone and ran to the car. I hauled out that trusty shotgun and leaned it against the car. I stood in front of it to hide it. It was nighttime, so it wasn't very hard to hide. About fifteen young guys came up, and as they approached me, I could see quite a few bicycle chains come out of some back pockets; they must have wanted to whip me pretty bad.

Jerry started to tell me how it was time someone showed me I wasn't that tough. When I brought the shotgun out from behind me and asked who was going to be first, boy, you should have seen the look on their faces. They rolled up their chains and put them back in their pockets. Jerry started stuttering when he told me they just wanted to talk and not fight. One Texan behind Jerry whispered, "Este vato esta pendejo y nos va matar." In English, this means "This guy is crazy, and he is going to kill us."

One of the guys with me convinced me to put the gun away and asked the Loveland boys who wanted to fight me clean, man to man. They all wanted me, but they settled on Ralph Compos, a weight lifter about my age but a heck of a lot bigger. They asked me if I would fight him one-on-one so that we could avoid a big gang fight. I knew that kid could knock the hell out of me, but I didn't show any signs of nervousness and said, "Yah, I'll fight him." Well, that pour kid never knew what hit him because when he started to take his coat off. I popped him over the head with a motorcycle chain. Dazed, he dropped down on his knees. The chain slipped out of my hand when I hit the poor guy, so I went at him with my fist and feet to finish the job. That started a big brawl. We came out ahead because the Loveland guys took off after we beat a few of them up. They also figured I was crazy enough to pull the shotgun out and shoot one of them. They were probably right.

In the next two years, I found myself in jail a couple of times for fighting. One night in Loveland, I beat up a guy; and consequently, I was sent to jail for two months for assault and battery. Three weeks later, I got out and ran into the same guy and his brother. I beat him up again and went right back to jail for another two months. Another time I was in a fight with Louis Espinoza, and we broke a big plate window in the Shamrock Tavern. We both spent Thanksgiving weekend in jail. Two brothers from Loveland, Gilbert and Albert Ornelas, didn't like me. So one night in Johnstown, I went at them with a billy club, and again I found myself in jail for assault and battery. I was a skinny kid and weighing 125 pounds and not strong and tough at all. I just thought it was fun to be in a fight.

During one night in Loveland, four of us boys from Johnstown got in a scuffle with a group of boys from Loveland. One of the guys from Loveland didn't like the fact he was smacked a few times by some of us, so he filed assault and battery charges against Herman, Sammy, and me. The day we went to court; the judge told us the charges against us were assault and battery and that the accuser would tell his side of the story, then we would have a chance to tell our side and cross-examine the accuser. The judge called for Sammy and asked if he was guilty or not. Sammy pleaded guilty, and then Herman did the same. The judge fined each one forty-five dollars plus court costs.

When I got up, the judge asked me the same question whether I was guilty or not. I said, "Not guilty," and asked if I could question the accuser a couple of questions. The judge said, "Go ahead." I asked the guy, "Was it day or night when you got smacked around?" This incident did occur during the night. I also asked how many people were there at the time, and he answered, "Six or eight." Then

I asked where the nearest street light was. He replied, "At the end of the alley about half a block away." My final question was "wouldn't it be safe to say that in a group scuffle like that night that if you got smacked in the face, your first instinct is to close your eyes?" He admitted, "Yes." My next response was "you really don't know if it was me that smacked you because it was at night, and you closed your eyes." He didn't respond, so I sat down. The judge looked at me and said, "Not guilty. Case dismissed." I should have gone to law school. Sammy and Herman were upset because we were all guilty, but they had to pay a fine, and I didn't.

In 1956, we thinned beets for a farmer north of Johnstown and lived near the Martin family. My sister Beatrice, whom we called Betty, was born that year. Mr. Martin had five beautiful daughters and a seventeen-year-old son. The son was a very sharp dresser, drove a red convertible, and had the reputation of being the best mambo dancer in the area. I kind of envied him, but more importantly, I was trying to find a way to date his sister Hilda. The parents were very protective with their daughters and went everywhere together. I never did get a chance to ask her for a date.

Anyhow, I don't think my girlfriend, Vicky, would have approved of it. She and I went together for a couple of years and occasionally talked about marriage. Her dad and my dad figured we would get married, and they called each other *compadres*. That is something couple's parents called each other when their children marry. When I went into the army, she didn't wait and married some guy from Loveland I used to fight with.

"Our family picture with my mom, Maria; sisters, Nena, Pinnie, Margie; brothers, Jimmy and Raymond."

"Dad and Mom, Candelario and Maria in 1958 standing by their home. This picture was sent to me while I was in the military stationed in Germany."

# CHAPTER 5

# The Adolescent Years of My Life

*Cada gallo canta en su gallinero.*

By midsummer, Dad decided to move to another farmhouse so that we could dig potatoes. In the process of moving, I got drunk on a couple of half pints of whisky that Archie Quintana and I stole from a liquor store. Dad was drinking some cheap wine and didn't realize Archie and I were also drinking. On the way to the other farmhouse, I was driving the truck loaded with our furniture. I hit a gravel spot on the road and lost some furniture off the truck. Mom was furious because she knew I was drinking; she called me a *borracho,* a drunk and a "sunamaviche" and looked for something to hit me with. She probably and justifiably wanted a baseball bat, but all she could find was a little tiny stick. She swatted me a couple of times on my arms, and in my drunken state, I felt humiliated and ashamed. I started running down the road into town, and right then, I decided to hitchhike to Amarillo. I asked a couple of friends to give me a ride to the highway so I could start walking toward Denver.

I stood there on the highway near the Berthoud turn off and stuck my thumb out until I got a ride. The man asked where I was going, so I told him Amarillo. As we traveled toward Denver, he was making conversation, and I told him I was in the navy and hitchhiking home on leave. When he asked me what my rank was, I told him I was a private. He didn't talk too much after that. When we got to Denver, he dropped me off on Colfax and told me to walk east to get back on the highway. He also told me that he was a sailor and that I was a liar. He said, "There's no such rank as private in the navy, so get out of my car."

Walking down the street toward the edge of town, still kind of drunk, I wondered if I would get a ride during the late night. It was close to midnight, and there was hardly any traffic. A police car went by, and when the officer saw me, he turned the car around and stopped where I was walking. He rolled a window down, shined a spot light on me, and asked me where I was going. I don't know what made me say it, but I told him, "No comprendo Engles, señor." He got out of the car and asked me some more questions, but I kept saying "no comprendo" to everything he asked. Finally in desperation, he put me in the car, and we drove to the Aurora, Colorado, police station. At the station, he and another policeman asked more questions, and I still kept saying "no comprendo." I heard one of them say to the other, "I know this little son of a bitch knows how to speak English as well as I do." After a while, they gave up and put me in jail.

The next morning, I was taken into a room, and another policeman brought me coffee and a roll. They brought in a Chicano who informed me that he was an interpreter. The policeman told the Chicano to inform me that he was going to ask a few questions. I started thinking maybe I should tell the truth, but then I thought if I did, I would probably get in real trouble, and maybe I would be sent to reform school.

The policeman told the interpreter what to ask me, and he would ask me in Spanish. So by the time the question got to me, I had a padded answer ready. I told them my name was *Carlos Salazar*. *I was fifteen years old and I was from a small village outside of Torreon, Coahuila. I was an orphan, lived with my grandmother, and herded sheep and goats for her. I had crossed into the United States near Juarez about two months ago and had hitched to Denver. No, I didn't have a passport to be in this country, and I understood I would have to go back to Mexico.*

I was put back in a jail cell, and in the afternoon, two men from immigration came and picked me up to take me downtown to the customs office. They didn't speak Spanish, except for a few words like "hombre and si," words that they probably learned in high school. At the immigration office, they took my picture and fingerprints and then drove me out to Stapleton Airport. Listening to them talk, I understood I was going to El Paso, Texas, by airplane, and then the plane would make a stop in Albuquerque. I had relatives there. I figured that would be my chance to get away and stop this foolishness. I wasn't a *wetback* like they thought, and I didn't want to be deported to Mexico.

I had never been on an airplane, so at the airport, I was fascinated by all of the planes that were coming in and taking off. When it came time for us to board, we walked out to the plane and up the ramp. At the top of the ramp, a nice-looking stewardess asked to see my boarding pass. I turned around and looked at one of the immigration officers. He explained to her that I was a wetback being deported to Mexico and that I didn't speak a word of English. She then smiled and started to show me to my seat. She said, "Oh, you don't speak English." I forgot myself and answered no. Instantly, I realized my mistake and felt a hot flash go over me. I thought now the immigration men would know I understood English. But they didn't catch on. I was excited that I was going to take my first airplane ride.

Passengers were getting on, and every time the stewardess went by, she would smile at me. We started to taxi down the runway when I saw a sign light up saying, "Please fasten seat belts and no smoking." I thought, "Oh, oh." If I fasten my seat belt, she's going to know I read English. I was getting a little panicky, but at the last minute, she came and fastened the belt for me. When we were in the air, she served us dinner, and I ate my tray clean. I hadn't eaten in twenty-four hours, except for a jelly roll and coffee. After dinners, as all the passengers sat back to read and relax; I sat there thinking of my predicament and how I was going to make a run for it when we stopped in Albuquerque.

The stewardess came by once and said, "Honey, you must be bored," so she got a Life magazine and put it on my lap. She flipped a few pages and said, "Pretty pictures, see the pretty pictures." I answered, "Oh si, señora, gracias." She left, and I thought if she knew I spoke and read as well as her, she would probably slap me on the side of my head for making a *tonta* (dummy) out of her.

We stopped in Albuquerque, but I didn't get a chance to run off like I had planned to. I thought maybe I'd get a chance in El Paso. I got to El Paso, but there were two guys in uniform from the border patrol waiting as I got off the plane. They asked me where I had been caught, and I told them in Denver. They took me to a detention center surrounded by barbed wire where there were other wetbacks that had been caught all over the country. Before they took me into barracks and assigned me a bunk, they told me to take my shirt off and drop my pants. One guy had a spray can of DDT fly spray, and he sprayed me all over to kill any body lice I might have. They gave me an old ragged army blanket and put me in the compound and told me to find a bunk in one of the buildings.

There must have been forty or fifty wetbacks, some sitting on the ground outside the barracks and about twenty of them lying on bunks. They were a rough-looking bunch and scared the hell out of me by just staring at me as I walked by. I tried not to show it by swaggering in and acting like I knew what I was doing and had been there before.

After a while, one of them asked me for a cigarette. I gave him one; and when I did, about twenty guys stood up, all wanting a cigarette. I just took one out for me and gave them the whole pack. I think that little gesture saved me because then, a few of them asked where I had been caught, and they introduced themselves and asked me my name.

I found an empty bunk, laid out my blanket, and sat down and thought, "Man, what am I doing here? I don't belong here with these wetbacks. I should be home in Johnstown with my family." I was scared and wanted to go home. Right then, I almost went out and told the guard that I was an American citizen. But I thought if I did, I would probably have to pay for the plane ride and go to jail for impersonating a *wetback*.

Two young guys in their late teens came up and told me they also had been caught in Denver and planned to go back. They asked what I intended to do, and I told them I would probably go back to Colorado. One of them suggested we go together, and I saw my chance of going home without having to go to jail and pay for the plane ride, so I said, "OK." Then I confessed to them that I was not a Mexican, nor a wetback, but a native-born American. They were amazed and thought I was nuts when I told them how I lied to the police and immigration to get in the predicament I was in. They thought it was great that I spoke English because once we went back across the border into the United States, I could do all the talking.

That evening, about ten o'clock, a guard came into the barracks and told forty-five of us to go outside and get in a big bus. It was a regular school bus, except for the metal bars on the windows to keep people from breaking out. We rode all night, and about sunup the next day, we arrived in Presidio, Texas. The bus stopped at a place near the Rio Grande River, and the guards gave each one of us a peanut butter and jelly sandwich and an orange for breakfast.

When we got off the bus, we were escorted to a bridge. We walked into a town called Ojinaga, Mexico, a small dusty little border town with unpaved streets and a few adobe houses and stores. At the railroad depot in Ojinaga, we waited a couple of hours for a passenger train to take us to the city of Chihuahua. There were no guards with us then because we were in the middle of the desert with no place to run. I could have sneaked across the border into the United States and started hitchhiking to Colorado, but I figured that I would have to pay for an airplane ride, and for now, I only had to pay for a bus ride. As we were walking through town toward the train depot, a dog halfheartedly barked at us and fell back asleep while a couple of old men sitting in the shade waved at us.

After a two-hour wait for the train, we go on and took off toward the city of Chihuahua. We arrived after a slow nine-hour ride through the desert, which was the end of the free ride for all *wetbacks*.

My two companions and I went to a cheap restaurant to eat, then we rented a room with three small beds. One of the guys went out to get laundry soap so we could wash our clothes because none of us had anything to change into. I asked him to get me a post card to send home to inform Mom where I was and tell her I was OK. I just couldn't think of what to say to her on the small card, so I just said, "Having fun, wish you were here."

A couple of days later, we decided it was time to head north to Juarez and on into the United States. We were almost broke and had about $5 between the three of us. We hitchhiked and finally got to Juarez the following morning. We loafed around all day and night then went down to the Rio Grande about two in the morning to hop a freight train out of El Paso. The only problem was that we bought two bottles of tequila, got drunk, and passed out while waiting for the freight train.

I woke up and had one nickel in my pocket. I told my two friends I had had enough of Mexico, and I was leaving for Colorado right then. They told me I wouldn't get far before the border patrol would catch me. I think they forgot that I was an American and not Mexican. I said good-bye and went across the river and crawled over a chain link fence with barbed wire on top. I started hitchhiking north to Las Cruces, New Mexico, and figured if a patrolman stopped me, I would speak the best English he had ever heard, and maybe they would help me get home. If not, then I'd go to Albuquerque, and then maybe my Aunt Socorro or her sons, Junior and Teo, would help me with bus fare to get home.

The first ride I got was with a bread delivery truck. When I told the two Chicanos in it where I had been, they gave me a couple of sandwiches from their lunch pails. They dropped me off in Las Cruces and gave me about thirty cents in change and said, "Have a good trip." Two rides later, one with an Indian family and one with an old cowboy, I was in Socorro, New Mexico, which was only eighty miles to go to get to Albuquerque. It was getting dark, and I thought nobody picks up hitchhikers at night, and all I had was a nickel in my pocket. I was hungry, so I bought a candy bar for supper and prayed somebody would give me a ride. Finally, a soldier from Fort Bliss picked me up; and luckily, he was going to Albuquerque. Hallelujah, my adventure as a wetback, and hitchhiker was over once I got to Albuquerque and my aunt or cousins loaned me the money for bus fare home. I had it made in the shade as we used to say.

My aunt couldn't give me money until payday, so I had to wait around a few days before I could take off for Colorado. One day, this kid Peewee and I went downtown just to look around and kill time. While we were walking back home, we stopped at a used car lot, and he went into the office to get a drink of water while I waited outside. When he came back, he was kind of excited and nervous. He told me to stand by the door going into to the office and keep a lookout for anyone coming. I said OK, wondering what he was up to, and stood by the door watching. He went behind a counter in the front office and picked up a little money box and came back out. We both took off like bullets. We ran home, and in the garage, we opened up the box and found over $400. I was so scared I couldn't talk straight and was shaking like a leaf in a windstorm. I pictured FBI men with machine guns looking for two teenage boys at train depots, bus stations, and airports.

I heard a siren that turned out to be an ambulance, but man, I was shitting bricks. I quickly went to my aunt's house and changed into different clothes that belonged to Teo. My half of the money amounted to about $230, and when I told my cousins what we had done, they immediately told me I owed them for room and board. I shoved a couple of twenties toward them and took off for the Greyhound bus station. I put all but $15 of the money in my shoes and bought a ticket to Greeley for $11. I finally quit shaking when I got to Greeley the next day.

I called Sammy Gonzalez and Jessie Molinar and asked if they'd come pick me up and give me a ride home. On the way home, we stopped at a liquor store, and Sam and Jessie pulled their change out of their pockets to pitch in for a six-pack. I pulled out my wad of bills and very nonchalantly said, "This one is on me, boys." Their eyes bugged out, and on the way home, I told them about my trip and how I had come into so much money.

I went to the house we moved to when I ran away, but Mom and Dad were at my Uncle Jose Quintana's house visiting. I hugged my brothers and sisters and asked Dolores if my folks were mad. She said they were worried about me but that as soon as they saw me and saw that I was OK, I'd probably catch hell. I went over to my uncle's house where they were visiting, and when I walked in, Mom got up and hugged me, and Dad kind of smiled and shook my hand and asked how I was doing. I told them I was fine and briefly told them where I was and what I did. Then I asked Dad if I could borrow his car and if he had any money so I could put gas in it. I was just going to give him some money, but I had to make a little production out of it.

When he reached in his pocket and pulled out about sixty cents in change, he apologized for not having more because he hadn't worked. I pulled out my money and told him, "Here, I have got some, hold your hand out." I proceeded to count out and hand him about $150. He was stunned; he looked at me in the eye then the money in his hand, and as he put it in his pocket, he asked where I had gotten it. I told him I had found a money bag that had probably fallen out of some car—near Truth or Consequences. I rehearsed this story over and over again, and I thought it was a good, believable story. He smiled, and I took off with my friends, happy to be home again and anxious to tell them about my adventure. Dad never questioned me about the money again, but many years later after he had passed away, Mom told me that he never believed the "cock and bull" story of me finding that money.

The rest of that year I not only fought with the Ornelases and Gonzalezes from Loveland but also had to fight pimples. I tried some remedies and doctor prescriptions, but nothing seemed to help. On the suggestion of an old man I met in jail, I drank a cup of hot water every morning as soon as I got out of bed, and that helped to get rid of them.

I worked for farmers in the area for a dollar an hour stacking hay or weeding corn. During the potato harvest, I got a job at the potato dock bagging one-hundred-pound sacks. I weighed one hundred twenty-five pounds myself, so it was pretty tough to wrestle the sacks into railroad cars and semitractors. I ate lunch down at the Dew Drop Inn, and for eighty cents, I could buy a chicken fried steak with all the trimmings. I bought myself a 1946 Ford with fender skirts and a shiny new black paint job that I was very proud of. I paid for it with hard-earned money, so I took pretty good care of it. It tickled the heck out of me when Dad's car wouldn't run, and he had to ask to borrow mine. I wouldn't lend it to him when he was drinking, but that son of a gun was good at hot wiring it with a copper penny and would take it sometimes.

In March 1957, we moved again. This time, we went east of Milliken to thin beets for Alex Betz. I was tired of moving and working in the fields and made plans to go into the navy in July when I turned seventeen. I dreamed of faraway places to visit and figured the military was the only way to get away from field work and change my lifestyle. I didn't have a good future as a civilian. In those days, a high school diploma was necessary for a good job, and all I had was six grades of formal education. If it hadn't been for Mom, it would have been less because of our moving so much. We would leave school in April or May before school let out and start school in the fall around October or November. Therefore, we never got report cards or passed from grade to grade. Every time we started at a school, she would tell us and the school what grade we were in. This way, she would pass us each year and keep us in our proper grade. I guess you could call her our "Board of Education."

GG got hit by a car in July and had to go to the hospital with a broken arm and hip bone. He got on his bike one Saturday and was going into town to buy candy when someone hollered at him. He turned around on the road without looking for cars and got hit. My sister Dolores and Sonny were married about then, and all the *padrino* and *mardina's* wedding party went to the hospital to visit him.

I was one of the *padrinos* and escorts and had to rent a tuxedo with a white dinner jacket. I drank quite a bit of wine and spilled some on the coat. I ruined it and had to buy it. I did the same thing years later in John Meza's wedding, and also, at my sister-in-law Jessie Feltz's wedding, I paid for three ruined tuxedos on account of drinking.

One Saturday night in Johnstown, I saw the Ornelas brothers and their cousin and beat on them with a billy club. A few days later,

I was out in a field working with Mom and Dad when the county sheriff came and arrested me; I was charged with assault and battery. I was put in jail in Johnstown, and I had a hunch I was going to the reform school in Golden. On my behalf, I convinced my friends to bring the Ornelas boys to the jail so I could talk to them. I was so mad at them for calling the police every time we fought that I threatened to kill them when I got out. My message must have been convincing because they dropped the charges and released. Tired of going to jail for fighting with them so much, I decided to never bother them again.

# CHAPTER 6

# Rites of Passage and Off to the Army

*Cada chango en su culumpio.*

When I turned seventeen, I tried joining the navy, but I failed the test. I just couldn't answer the math questions. The navy recruiter suggested I try the air force or the army. Archie Quintana decided to join the air force with me, so we signed up. He didn't pass the physical exam, and I forgot to list one of the times I was in jail and tried to tell them at the swearing-in ceremony. They sent me home and told me to get five letters of character reference, and then they would let me in. After arriving home, I got the letters but was later told that there was a three-month waiting list to get in the air force.

Meanwhile, Dad and I were not getting along very well on account of his drinking. He was either really drunk or hung over, and I was losing respect for him. I really loved the man, but I wanted us to have a normal family life like my friends. We moved into the town of Milliken to be near the potato dock where Mom, Dad, and I got jobs for the potato harvest. We live one month in that two-room house and then moved again. Dad thought it was ridiculous to pay $20 a month for rent, so we went to a farmhouse west of Johnstown.

Dad and I wouldn't speak to each other for weeks, and Mom would try to reconcile our differences; this occurred a couple of years later after I gave Dad $150 cash at age fifteen. I made a comment once to Mom about how I wished Dad was a better man, and she got mad. She said I shouldn't talk like that because a statement like that could come back to haunt me.

I kept hoping that the air force would call me so I could leave and get away from home. I planned to make a career of the service because what future did I have without an education? I didn't want to be a migrant and a poor man the rest of my life.

One day in September, I was walking in downtown Greeley and saw an army recruiting sign. Out of curiosity, I walked in. The sergeant in the office smiled real friendly and asked if I was interested in joining the army. I answered, "No, I'm going into the air force in a couple of weeks." He told me if I joined the army, I'd go to Germany. I asked when I could leave, and he said right away, so I joined the army. Two weeks later, I was on my way to Fort Benning, Georgia.

Instead of going into the infantry like I was told, I was assigned to a tank unit. On my application, I lied and said I worked for a construction company and that I went to high school in Amarillo. That's the reason I got into the tank unit. Tank is nothing more than an oversized caterpillar with a cannon and machine guns.

It's funny that every soldier complained about army chow, but I thought it was great. I was eating roast beef, mashed potatoes, and vegetables and drinking all the milk I wanted instead of frijoles, papas, tortillas, beans, and potatoes. In six weeks, I steadily gained weight and went from a 125-pound weakling to a 145 "Charles Atlas," or so I thought.

I didn't get to go home for Christmas, so a friend of mine invited me to spend the holidays with his family in Georgia. I was kind of bitter that I hadn't been able to go home in my new uniform. I wanted to brag to my friends about the good time in the army. One night, I was drinking beer in the PX and got drunk and was homesick. I was in the army five months and thought, "The heck with it." I got on a Greyhound bus and went home. AWOL, Mom and the kids were happy to see me, and I was glad to be home. I told her I had a thirty-day furlough.

Dad had been in California and also came home about the same time. He had lost an eye in a bar room fight, and I felt sorry for him. He didn't drink while I was home, and we had a wonderful time. Dad died in an accident two years later when I was in Germany, so I never saw him again. It was an odd death where he was sleeping in a sheepherder's wagon when a cigarette caused the cotton mattress to burn. Consequently, he, the sheepherder, and the two dogs died from smoke inhalation. Dad was only thirty-nine years old.

After thirty days, I told the folks my leave was up. I went to Denver and gave myself up to the military police, and they sent me back to Fort Benning. I got a court martial, and my sentence was a suspended five months in jail and $50 out of my pay for five months. My pay was only $72 a month, so it was going to be rough for the five months.

My unit was shipped to Germany, and when we got there, they transferred me to an infantry unit. In the process, they lost my records, so I didn't have to pay the fine either. I got in trouble five more times before I settled down. I tried to beat up three military policemen, went AWOL, and fought with other GIs.

When I settled down, I don't know how or what made me do it. I was made a corporal and a squad leader. They made me "Soldier of the Month" one year and "Colonel's Orderly" a couple of times. I even had an appointment to the Noncommissioned Officers Academy in Munich.

I sent Mom a $50 savings bond every month, so I didn't have too much money left out of a $160 a month paycheck. I visited Paris, London, Frankfurt, and other cities in Europe, but the most important discovery in my life was the library. I would go to the library to hide from the sergeants so as not to have to do any work, and I enjoyed reading. I spent hours reading books by John Steinbeck, Zane Grey, and Mark Twain. I also read books on basic math, history, and Dr. Kinsey's book on human sexuality.

I lived on a budget of $20 a week, which wasn't bad because the army provided all of my needs. Cigarettes cost twelve cents a pack, and a sixteen-ounce mug of excellent German beer cost fifteen cents. On payday, my roommate and I would go downtown and eat a nice dinner with wine and all the trimmings for a dollar-fifty!

In 1959, Elvis Presley was drafted into the army and was sent to Germany. He was stationed forty miles down the road from me, but I never went down to see him. I liked his music, but I was more into listening to *black music*. My favorites were Little Richard, the Platters, Sam Cooke, the Coasters, and Fats Domino.

When I enlisted into the service, I had a girlfriend that I planned to marry when I got out. I hated army life, so I couldn't make a career out of it and decided to work in road construction for my girlfriend's dad. One day, she quit writing to me, and I couldn't understand why I wasn't getting any mail from her. My sister, Dolores, wrote me a letter and informed me that my girl had gotten married. I was stunned at first then got angry. I ripped up her pictures and letters and burned them in the incinerator. It wasn't unusual for a soldier to get a "Dear John" letter while he was overseas. A lot of them married

German girls not because they loved them but doing it out of spite of their ex-girlfriends to show them that they were fooling around too. Not me, forget that; I promised myself right then that I wouldn't get married until I was thirty years old.

I dated a few girls over there, but nothing serious. One was over there with her family because her dad was an army sergeant. They were Puerto Ricans, and I enjoyed her company because she spoke Spanish. One German girl was afraid to be seen with me because her family hated American soldiers.

# CHAPTER 7

# Finding My Way Back from the Army

*No me cole-es.*

In March of 1960, the Red Cross called me to their office and informed me that my dad had passed away. They didn't know the details of how he had died, but I was to leave immediately to try to be home in time for the funeral. I didn't cry or break down; I just went into a kind of trance. I was told to take all my belonging because I wouldn't be coming back to Germany. I said good-bye to my friends that afternoon, and at 8:00 p.m., I got on a flight from Frankfurt to the *U. S. of A.*

Arriving in Johnstown two days late on account of bad connections, I missed Dad's funeral by one day. My Uncle Nino, Fidel, and Sonny Derrera picked me up at the Denver airport, and on the way home, they informed me how Dad had died. He was drinking wine at a sheep herder's camper a half mile from where we lived. They both passed out from drinking too much. A burning cigarette fell on a cotton mattress, and it started smoldering. They and two sheep dogs died of smoke asphyxiation.

We knew why Dad was drinking with the sheep herder because he had done it before with other sheep herders. Sheep herders are lonely people, and Dad knew this one, so he would buy a bottle of wine and visit. After they both were good and drunk and in good spirits, Dad would talk him into giving him a lamb. They would load the lamb into the backseat of the car and laugh and joke about it like a couple of mischievous kids. Dad would take the lamb home and slaughter it to feed the family. During the winter months, when he couldn't find work, the welfare office would help him with about $25 a month to buy groceries. It wasn't enough, and he was trying to feed his family the best way he could. Dad was a very sick man most of his life, and we didn't know it. Even he didn't know he had a disease. The disease is known today as alcoholism.

I loved that man dearly as well as many other people. Wherever he went, he made friends easily and was well liked by everyone. He was a smart man that could do just about anything. He only went to the third grade, yet he could overhaul an automobile engine. He could build a house, carve furniture and toys, and if he had a pickup truck, he could create his own jobs. Had he lived a long, full life, he would have spoiled his grandchildren rotten. He worked in a restaurant as a cook when he was a young man and never lost his fondness for cooking. Sometimes he'd help Mom in the kitchen, and you could smell the aroma of fresh homemade bread and cinnamon rolls; a roast with potatoes au gratin or potatoes simmering in a tomato sauce. He'd cook wild spinach or asparagus and all those veggies that kids don't like until they grow up.

All of our relatives came up from New Mexico for Dad's funeral. I got to the house and saw Mom and all my brothers and sisters. I came to the realization that I was the head of the house now. I asked them to take me to the cemetery where Dad was buried, and when I saw the headstone, I broke down and cried.

I stayed home a month and helped Mom move into a small house she bought in Milliken. All those years of moving from house to house had finally come to an end. The army reassigned me to Fort Ord in California for the remaining nine months of my three-year hitch. I came home a couple of times on leave and with Siguel Velasquez and John Meza. We liked going to Fort Collins to party and attend dances.

I got out of the army in November of 1960 at the age of twenty and drew unemployment checks for a year. I partied and drank and had a good time trying to make up for what I missed while I was in the army. I bought a 1957 Mercury and drove it forty thousand in twelve months. I got a DUI ticket in that time, and Mom started telling me if I didn't control my drinking, I'd wind up like Dad. She threatened to throw me out of the house once when I was continuously drunk for two weeks.

On Sunday mornings, Mom and the kids would go to mass in Johnstown and have to drive with all the windows down to air out the car. There were empty beer bottles and cans left over from the night before.

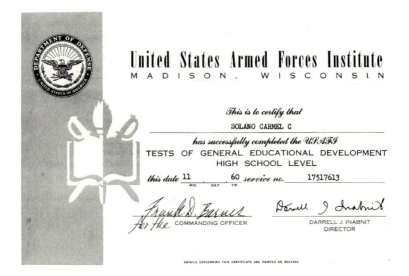

"My GED, an achievement that I wanted and received in 1960 through the United States Armed Forces Institute."

# CHAPTER 8

# Finding My Lifelong Friend and Moving On

*Otra vez el burro al maiz.*

One night at a party at Siguel's girlfriend's house, I saw my future wife for the first time. After that, I was always trying to scheme ways on how to take her out on a date. I finally got to take her home from a dance one Saturday night with two other couples who drove out to Richards Lake, a local lovers' lane located northeast of Fort Collins, Colorado. She kept pushing me off while I was trying to kiss and smooch her. I finally got tired and passed out. I finally finagled a date with her on Memorial Day in 1961, and with two other couples, we went on a picnic in Loveland. I dated Judy Barela for two years, and on October 5, 1963, she became my wife.

A week before I got out of the army, I took a GED test without ever going to class. The time I spent in the library in Germany paid off. After I got out of the army, the University of Wisconsin Testing Center sent me a letter stating I passed all five tests and sent me a high school GED certificate.

I worked in construction as a hod carrier for a while, hoping to become a bricklayer, but I saw it as hard work, and I scratched that idea fast.

In the winter of 1961, I packed a suitcase and left home for good. I went to Liberal, Kansas, and lived in the back of a gas station that had a cot for truckers to sleep overnight. I teamed up with Abby Velasquez and headed for California. It took us about three weeks to get to Los Angeles, and we lived on beef jerky and beer and slept in the car most of the time. We were drunk much of the time and partied all along the way. We got drunk in Dalhart, Texas, Tucumcari, and Albuquerque, New Mexico, and finally got to Los Angeles with sixty cents between us.

My cousin Johnnie Velasquez was moving to Denver from Los Angeles and was bringing two Mr. Softie Ice Cream trucks. I offered to drive one for him if he would feed me, and that is how I ended up in Denver.

I moved in to an apartment with an old buddy, nicknamed Squirrel. John Meza and I shared an apartment until he got drafted when I moved to Arvada, Colorado. In 1962, I spent part of the summer down in Alamogordo and Chama, New Mexico, as a foreman for a telephone pole inspection company that belonged to Johnnie Velasquez and Bob Foster. I came back to Denver in midsummer and started driving one of their Mr. Softie Ice Cream trucks on the streets of Denver.

Judy and I were engaged a few months and saw her more often. On weekends, I traveled to Fort Collins by bus, or she would come to Denver with a couple of friends, and we went dancing at the Blue Blaze in north Denver. She didn't like Mexican music. She was more of a country western music fan. She eventually learned to like Mexican music.

One weekend when Squirrel and I were roommates, Judy and Teresa Roybal came to Denver, and Squirrel and I got pretty loaded. After dancing and drinking all night, they took us to our apartment and dropped us off. We went in and passed out right away. The girls headed back to Fort Collins, but their car stalled in the parking lot. They banged on our apartment door but couldn't wake us up. They woke up our landlady, and she told them to cut out the racket. The girls decided to rent a room across the street from our apartment. The next morning, they called us and told us what happened and why they were still in town. We met them in a coffee shop for breakfast then went and got their car started. They were shocked and embarrassed when we told them they had spent the night in a hotel where homosexuals or gays congregated. They also accused us of going into our apartment the night before and sneaking out the back door to continue to party. It wasn't true, but since we didn't answer the door, they never believed us.

In the winter of 1962, I found myself in a tight spot with no job or money. I couldn't draw unemployment benefits because the guy I worked for paid cash, so neither of us wouldn't have to claim income tax. My rent money ran out, and I had to move out of the apartment in Arvada. Tony Meza, Squirrel's brother, had an apartment in Denver; and I asked if I could crash for a week. I promised Tony that if by the end of the week I couldn't find work, I would leave Denver and move back to Milliken. I didn't want to do that without having any money because I used to like to go home and visit Mom and the kids only when I was in the chips when I could give her some money. To me, if I went home broke and hungry, I was admitting defeat, and I was not able to look after myself. Besides, Mom was dating Secundino Lobato, and we could hear wedding bells in the air for them.

For a week, I pounded the streets of Denver looking for work and living on a cup of coffee and sweet roll per day. Tony was going to barber school at the time, and he suggested I go to the state rehabilitation and see if they would pay my way through school. They were paying his way plus room and board but only because he was an ex-convict. When I applied at the State Office of Rehabilitation, they asked what my handicap was. They tore up my application when I answered "lack of funds."

In the want-ad section of the *Rocky Mountain News*, all I could see were ads for barbers and dishwashers. So I thought OK, if that's what is needed, then that is what I'll do. I applied for a job at Trader Vic's restaurant and started bussing tables. When I applied for the job, the manager, Leo Goto, told me my duties and that my pay would be $1.09 an hour, plus one meal a day and if I had any questions. My only question was "When do we eat?" He asked if I was hungry, and when I told him I hadn't had a meal in a week, he went to the cook and fixed me a plate of food. I ate right there in his office.

I started working at Trader Vic's in November of 1962 and enrolled in Colorado Barber College on Larimer Street. The waiting list of persons wanting to go to barber school was so long I would have to wait till the following March before I could start school. The tuition was $300; the tools cost $120. It would take me six months to finish the course. The school allowed me to pay them in monthly installments of $71.

I was paying Zales Jewelers $20 a month for Judy's engagement ring, Gambles department store $20 a month, and my hotel room $46 a month. My income was $190.40, plus tips, and my expenses were $157.00. That left me with about $34 extra a month to eat and save for my wedding that was coming up in October, only six months away.

*Life ain't easy*, to whoever is reading this, but nobody ever told me it was. But always remember this: you can do anything you want to do if you set your mind to do it.

What really helped me was a comment my sister Dolores's mother-in-law made when I went home to visit Mom and the kids for Christmas. Mom was married that summer to Secundino Lovato, and I wanted to meet him. Dolores told me that when she mentioned to her mother-in-law that I was to become a barber, her only comment was that I wouldn't do it because Mexicanos never finish what they start. Two of her sons had started an electronic course and never finished, so she figured I'd do the same. That was all I needed for incentive because come hell or high water, I had to prove to her that I could do it. I never forgot that comment, and for the rest of my life, it has gotten me through many rough times. "Thank you, Mrs. Derrera."

I worked in the restaurant from 6:00 p.m. to 2:00 a.m. With other bus boys or waiters, I would go bowling at Celebrity Lanes or play cards until 5:00 a.m. I'd sleep during the day until 3:00 p.m., and then go to work. In one month's time, I lost twenty-five pounds and started to lose a lot of hair. I was a walking zombie and was constantly tired. Sometimes in school, I'd go to the bathroom, and the instructor had to pound on the door because I had fallen asleep in the *john*.

One Saturday morning, I overslept and got to school three hours late. The instructor was mad, so as a form of punishment, he told me to stay out of school for a week. That meant it would take a week longer to graduate. To me, that was a very much-needed vacation. I took advantage of it, and for that whole week, all I did was sleep.

One of the bus boys I worked with was a *pothead* who smoked marijuana every day. He suggested I smoke some at the restaurant and I would feel better and the night would go by faster. It was a disaster because it made me forget simple orders from the waiter and distorted my sense of time. Things I thought took hours only took minutes, and I zoomed around the dining room like a roller coaster. It seemed like forever before that shit wore off, and I never tried that again.

For some reason, people like to steal things from restaurants. Our customers were no different. Trader Vic's was a first-class restaurant with fancy china and fine linen. I met Louis Armstrong, the jazz musician, and I met Kitty and Doc from the old *Gunsmoke* show. I also met Fred and Faye, a local couple that did a children's television show, and William Bendix from the old *Life of Riley* comedy show.

Wealthy couples came to the restaurant; and when they had a few drinks, they would put ashtrays, silverware, menus, or even lamps in their pockets or purses. Women were the worst offenders. If I spotted them before the waiter did, I made out like a bandit. If I'd see a woman put an object in her purse, I'd approach her boyfriend and very discreetly tell him that his lady friend would have to put whatever she took back on the table or I would have to call the manager. To avoid any embarrassment, he would slip me $5 and whisper, "You didn't see anything, did you?" and I would say, "Not a thing, sir." Then I would go to the storeroom and replace the item that had been stolen.

Sometimes when customers left the waiter a big tip, I'd bus the table and hide part of his tip under a saltshaker or lamp; and when the coast was clear, I'd put it in my pocket. I had an upcoming wedding, school tuition, room and board, and an engagement ring to pay for; so I did what I had to do. Many a time I felt like quitting barber school, but I would remember what Mrs. Derrera had said, and I was going to prove her wrong.

Judy and I got married in October of 1963 about the same time I finished barber school. We went to Denver to live. We had no money for a honeymoon trip. I didn't start my first job for a week, so we just saw the sights in Denver.

Mom and her second husband loaned us a black 1949 Chevrolet for a couple of weeks to get around. We lived in Denver for about a month. Judy didn't like living in the city, and I was only making about $60 a week at my first job as a barber. We moved to Fort

Collins to be near the university where I could make more money cutting students' hair.

We moved in with my in-laws, Manuel and Mary Barela, for two weeks until we found a house we could rent. We moved in to my brother-in-law's house and paid $65 a month rent. I needed transportation, so I bought a 1949 Mercury for $150. I gave the man $50 for a down payment and financed the rest for six months. My father-in-law was my cosigner.

Our first daughter was born ten months after our wedding day, and with no insurance, we had to pay about $400. It took about three years to pay it off. Judy got sick after giving birth to April and stayed with her parents for a couple of weeks so her mom could look after her while I worked. My in-laws weren't a drinking family, and I was, so there were conflicting views at first. One night I partied with Dick Maxwell, Judy's cousin, whom I worked with, and went to see Judy at 3:00 a.m.

We had our first argument, and her mother sided up with her. It was tense for a couple of days because Judy wouldn't talk to me on the phone when I called. I was told that she had talked to a lawyer about a divorce. I resented my mother-in-law for not letting me talk to Judy. Whenever I called, she would be so sarcastically sweet and nice. She would tell me that Judy wasn't home. I knew she was because I had just driven by their house and seen Judy's car. On one of these occasions, I got angry and called my mother-in-law an "old busybody" and hung up on her.

After a couple of days, I finally got Judy to talk to me and made arrangements to go see her. No sooner had I walked into her mother's house than her mother attacked me with a kitchen broom. As she was hitting me, I began to back out of the kitchen door trying to ward off the blows with my arms. She said, "You son of a bitch, don't ever call me a busybody, etc. . . . ." I left her house humiliated and embarrassed. Judy and I eventually overcame our differences, and she came home, but her mother and I didn't speak or visit each other for about two years. I finally went and apologized, and in time, we became real good friends. Up to this day, friends and relatives laugh when we remember the incident and say that I'm the only one who ever got beaten with a broom by his mother-in-law.

We rented our homes for a couple of years. We usually paid about $65 a month until finally, in 1967, we were able to buy a two-bedroom house for $6,000. Our second daughter, Penny, was born in 1968; and our third daughter, Judy Junior, in 1971.

I opened one of the first men's hairstyling shops in Fort Collins in January of 1972. I was a success from the start. I charged $6.50 when others were charging $2.50, and I also shaved girls' legs at twenty-five cents a leg. I did it to get publicity, and sure enough, I got it. The local paper did an article on my shop and my services. The UPI wire service picked it up and showed the article and a picture of me shaving a girl's leg in newspapers all over the country. It raised a few hackles in local barbers, and the state barber board informed me that if I didn't stop, they would take away my shop license. I threatened to beat up the two barbers that were most against it because they even tried to have the reporter fired for writing the article. Since I got the publicity I wanted and everybody in town knew about my men's hairstyling shop, I just let it drop and didn't beat up anybody.

In 1972, we bought a brand-new three-bedroom house with an unfinished basement. We saved some money for a year so that we could finish the basement, but instead of finishing it, we used the money for a trip to Disneyland. I figured the kids would enjoy the trip to California more than the finished basement. In later years, they could say one of two things, "Boy, my dad really did a nice job of finishing the basement" or "We had a great time in California."

We've done a lot of things that I didn't have the opportunity to do when I was growing up. We didn't take a vacation every year in the next ten years, but I did manage to take them to California five times. Three times we drove and twice we went by airplane. I bought a camper and took them camping for a couple of summers, but they weren't too excited about it. We took a lot of short trips here in Colorado, and I think their idea of roughing it was a cabin in the mountain with all the comforts of home but with no television.

A few years earlier, I had been in the local chapter of the U.S. Jaycees, and they helped me a great deal on organizational work and public speaking. Hell, until I joined the Jaycees, I couldn't stand up in a public meeting and just give my name without breaking out in a cold sweat. I became vice president of our chapter of League of United Latin American Citizens. I finished out a term for Dr. Abel Amaya as chairman of the Chicano Advisory Committee for our school district. I was on the Human Relations Advisory Board for the city of Fort Collins. I was treasurer for Saint Joseph's School PTA. I was president of the Parks and Recreation Advisory Board for the city of Fort Collins, and I was a candidate for city council in 1978 but didn't get elected. I became a member of a twelve-step program in April 1981.

Through the technology of television, I've seen a man blast off into space and land on the moon, the assassination of President Kennedy, the shooting of his assailant Oswald by Jack Ruby, the eruption of Mount Saint Helens, the war in Vietnam, and the Denver Broncos in a Super Bowl game.

My brothers and sisters have created a lifestyle entirely different from the one they were raised in. After growing up on welfare, they have become secretaries, supervisors at IBM, teachers, college students at UNC, drywall contractors, and quality control inspectors. My mother became a teacher's aide for the school district in Johnstown. What better role for a lady who raised ten children. She saw us all hoeing a rough row of sugar beets and one day saw us get to the end of the row. We just kept on going to better and bigger things.

*I am an American.*

*I am a Manito.*

*I am a Mexican.*

*I am a Chicano.*

*My blood is native to the lands where I once picked the gifts from the earth.*

*My brow sweats the tears from my ancestors, who came before me and left their sweat and blood in the fields.*

*My hands are old from the hoe I carried around many years ago.*

Footnote:

This quote came from an unknown author that I modified to fit my belief.

—Chuck Solano

Edwards Brothers Malloy
Thorofare, NJ USA
April 3, 2013